Publications of the
CENTRE FOR REFORMATION AND RENAISSANCE STUDIES

SERIES EDITOR   KONRAD EISENBICHLER

Essays and Studies, 8

Victoria University
in the
University of Toronto

Sacrilege and Redemption

in Renaissance Florence

The Case of Antonio Rinaldeschi

WILLIAM J. CONNELL and GILES CONSTABLE

Toronto
Centre for Reformation and Renaissance Studies
2005

CRRS Publications
Centre for Reformation and Renaissance Studies
Victoria University in the University of Toronto
Toronto, Ontario M5S 1K7
Canada

Tel: 416/585–4465
Fax: 416/585–4430
Email: <crrs.publications@utoronto.ca>
<www.crrs.ca>

Library and Archives Canada Cataloguing in Publication

Connell, William J
     Sacrilege and redemption in renaissance Florence : the case of Antonio
Rinaldeschi / William J. Connell and Giles Constable.

(Essays and studies ; 8)
Includes bibliographical references and index.
ISBN 0-7727-2030-4

     1. Rinaldeschi, Antonio, d. 1501—Trials, litigation, etc. 2. Trials
(Sacrilege)—Italy—Florence—History—16th century. I. Constable, Giles
II. Victoria University (Toronto, Ont.). Centre for Reformation and
Renaissance Studies III. Title. IV. Series: Essays and studies (Victoria
University (Toronto, Ont.). Centre for Reformation and Renaissance
Studies) ; 8

DG738.14.R55C65 2005 345.45'0288   C2005-904208-7

Cover illustration: Filippo Dolciati, *The History of Antonio Rinaldeschi*,
Museo Stibbert, Florence. By permission of the Museo Stibbert.

Cover design: Ian MacKenzie, Paragraphics
Typesetting: Becker Associates

Contents

List of Illustrations 7

Archival Abbreviations 9

Foreword 11

A Note on Chronology 14

A Note on Currency 15

Chapter One: The Culprit and His Offences 17

Chapter Two: The Nature of the Offence 35

Chapter Three: The Context of Florentine History 51

Illustrations 73

Appendix of Documents

    I. The sentence of the Eight for Security against
Antonio Rinaldeschi 101

    II. "Narration of the Crime of Rinaldesco," from the
account book of the *opera* of the Madonna de' Ricci,
in the hand of Giovanni Landi 104

    III. A notice from records kept by the Company of
the Blacks 107

    IV. A second notice from records kept by the Company of
the Blacks 108

    V. From the *Diary* of Luca Landucci 110

    VI. From a seventeenth-century miscellany compiled
by Carlo Strozzi 111

    VII. A record copied from a *priorista* that belonged to
Matteo Segaloni in 1630 113

VIII. Payments to the painter Filippo Dolciati in the
account book of the *opera* of the Madonna de' Ricci,
in the hand of Giovanni Landi   115

 IX. The decision of the *opera* to hire the architect Baccio
d'Agnolo to build a new oratory for the Madonna
de' Ricci   117

Index   121

LIST OF ILLUSTRATIONS

Figure 1.　Filippo Dolciati, *Rinaldeschi loses at dice.*

Figure 2.　*Rinaldeschi gathers dung.*

Figure 3.　*Rinaldeschi throws dung at the Virgin.*

Figure 4.　*The arrest of Rinaldeschi.*

Figure 5.　*Rinaldeschi taken to Florence.*

Figure 6.　*Rinaldeschi led from his cell.*

Figure 7.　*Examination by the Eight.*

Figure 8.　*Rinaldeschi's confession.*

Figure 9.　*The hanging of Rinaldeschi.*

Figure 10.　Filippo Dolciati, *The History of Antonio Rinaldeschi*. Florence, Museo Stibbert. Overall view.

Figure 11.　The sentence of the Eight for Security against Antonio Rinaldeschi. Archivio di Stato di Firenze, Otto di guardia e balìa, 120, fols. 128[r–v].

Figure 12.　*Image of Infamy on the Palace of the Podestà*, engraving by Vincenzo Cavini after a drawing by Giuseppe Manni. From Angelo Poliziano, *Conjurationis Pactianae anni MCCCCLXXVIII commentarium*, ed. G. Adimari (Naples, 1769), 139.

Figure 13.　Filippino Lippi, *St. Paul Visiting St. Peter in Prison*. Florence, Church of S. Maria del Carmine, Brancacci Chapel.

Figure 14.　Duccio di Buoninsegna, *Christ Taken Prisoner*. Siena, Museo dell'Opera del Duomo.

Figure 15.　Gallows and the chapel known as "The Temple." Detail from *Mappa della Catena*, circa 1470. Florence, Museo di Firenze com'era.

Figure 16.　Cover of the "Liber condemnationum" of Messer Monaldo de' Fascioli of Orvieto, Podestà of Florence in 1501, with his coat-of-arms. Archivio di Stato di Firenze, Atti del Podestà, 5547.

Figure 17.　Illustration from the Escorial Codex of the *Cantigas de Santa Maria* of Alfonso the Wise. Biblioteca de San Lorenzo el Real de El Escorial, codex T. I. 1, Cantiga 136, fol. 192[r].

Figure 18.   Illustration from the Florence Codex of the *Cantigas de Santa Maria* of Alfonso the Wise. Biblioteca Nazionale Centrale, Florence, Banco Rari 20, Cantiga 294, fol. 20^r.

Figure 19.   Illustration from the Escorial Codex of the *Cantigas de Santa Maria*. Biblioteca de San Lorenzo el Real de El Escorial, codex T. I. 1, Cantiga 154, fol. 209^r.

Figure 20.   Fra Bartolomeo. *Portrait of Girolamo Savonarola*. Florence, Museo di S. Marco.

Figure 21.   Anonymous artist, *The Execution of Savonarola and Two Followers in the Piazza of the Signoria, 23 May 1498*. Florence, Museo di S. Marco.

Figure 22.   View of S. Maria degli Alberighi, circa 1447. Florence, Biblioteca del Seminario Arcivescovile Maggiore di Cestello, codex of Marco di Bartolommeo Rustici.

Figure 23.   S. Maria degli Alberighi and the oratory constructed by Baccio d'Agnolo. Detail from the map of Florence by Stefano Buonsignori, *Nova pulcherrimae civitatis Florentiae topographia accuratissime delineata* (Florence, 1584).

Figure 24.   Florence, Church of the Madonna de' Ricci, façade on the Via del Corso.

Figure 25.   *Madonna de' Ricci*, detail of Figure 3.

Figure 26.   *Madonna de' Ricci*, fresco. Florence, Church of the Madonna de' Ricci, before restoration. From C. Torricelli, *La Chiesa della Madonna de' Ricci* (Florence, [1926]).

Figure 27.   *Madonna de' Ricci*, fresco. Florence, Church of the Madonna de' Ricci. Photograph taken 1995.

Figure 28.   *Annunziata*, panel painting. Florence, Church of the SS. Annunziata.

ARCHIVAL ABBREVIATIONS

The following abbreviations have been used in the notes:

ASF	=	Archivio di Stato, Florence
APTPS	=	Archivio della Provincia Toscana dei Padri Scolopi, Florence
Banc.	=	Bancroft Library, University of California, Berkeley
BNCF	=	Biblioteca Nazionale Centrale, Florence
NA	=	Notarile antecosimiano
OGB	=	Otto di guardia e balìa. Periodo repubblicano
PR	=	Provvisioni. Registri

FOREWORD

Our account of the crime committed by Antonio Rinaldeschi and of his punishment was previously published in a shorter form in the *Journal of the Warburg and Courtauld Institutes* in 1998.[1] Since then, the article has attracted more interest than is usual for an essay published in an academic journal. It was mentioned in the *New Yorker* magazine in an article on the history of dice and gambling.[2] An author from California wrote to say that he was retelling the Rinaldeschi episode in a novel for a major New York publisher. A theatre student in Arizona even sent an email asking if we objected to his writing a play about Rinaldeschi. (We did not.) Scholars, too, have been kind to the essay. Professor Nicholas Eckstein of the University of Sydney recently discussed it in an introductory article for a special issue of the *Journal of Religious History*.[3] We are especially grateful to Professor Oleg F. Kudriavtsev of Moscow State University, who wrote a lengthy and careful review of the article in Russian, which we have not been able to read, but which friends who know Russian have summarized for us.[4] Since considerations of space required the omission of some material when the essay was first published, and a number of matters have required updating, we are delighted now to be able now to publish the essay in its full form, and with illustrations in colour of the painting by Filippo Dolciati. inteeriotity infer

As an example of what Robert Darnton recently called "incident analysis,"[5] we believe the case of Antonio Rinaldeschi offers an unusually

---

[1] W. J. Connell and G. Constable, "Sacrilege and Redemption in Renaissance Florence," *Journal of the Warburg and Courtauld Institutes*, 61 (1998), 53–92.

[2] R. Jay, "The Story of Dice," *The New Yorker Magazine* (11 December 2000), 91–95.

[3] N. A. Eckstein, "Words and Deeds, Stasis and Change: New Directions in Florentine Devotion Around 1500," *Journal of Religious History*, 28:1 (February 2004), 1–18. See also E. S. Cohen and T. V. Cohen, *Daily Life in Renaissance Italy* (Westport, Conn., 2001), 281.

[4] O. F. Kudriavtsev, "Renessansnaia Florentsiia v neprivychnom aspekte: prestuplenie i nakazanie Antonio Rinaldeski," in *Dialog so vremenem: almanakh intellektualnoi istorii*, 6 (Moscow, 2001), 371–378.

[5] R. Darnton, "It Happened One Night," *New York Review of Books*, 51:11 (24 June 2004), 60–64.

revealing look into the cultural, political and religious forces at work in
Florence circa 1500. Although we have drawn on a wide range of
European sources and traditions, we have tended to emphasize documen-
tation from periods prior to the Rinaldeschi case as being more likely to
have informed the procedures, traditions and sentiments that came into
play in this episode. One subject we specifically did not address was the
contested relationship between religious piety and devotional images in
the Protestant Reformation. Protestant iconoclasm has been the subject
of a number of studies in recent decades.[6] Scholars who write about the
fifteenth through seventeenth centuries continue to explore the question
whether Protestant assaults on religious images and the increase in the
number of image-centred devotions in Catholic Europe were the mark-
ers of a thoroughgoing parting of the ways or were instead symptomatic
of a shared, profound anxiety in European culture about new modes of
representation and of what is sometimes awkwardly called "cultural
reproduction"—a term meant to comprise such things as the Renaissance
rediscovery of linear perspective and the development of the printing
press.[7] Certainly the history of Antonio Rinaldeschi's crime involving a
painting offers material relevant to this theme. As we argue below, much

---

[6] P. Mack Crew, *Calvinist Preaching and Iconoclasm in the Netherlands, 1544–1569*
(Cambridge, 1978); C. Eire, *War Against the Idols: The Reformation of Worship from
Erasmus to Calvin* (Cambridge, 1986); M. Warnke, "Durchbrochene Geschichte? Die
Bilderstürme der Widertäufer in Münster 1534/35," in *Bildersturm. Die Zerstörung des
Kunstwerks*, ed. M. Warnke (Frankfurt a.M., 1988), 65–98; L. P. Wandel, *Iconoclasm
in Reformation Zurich, Strasbourg, and Basel* (Cambridge, 1995); and the contributions
in *Macht und Ohnmacht der Bilder. Reformatorischer Bildersturm im Kontext der europäischen
Geschichte*, ed. P. Blickle, A. Holenstein, H. R. Schmidt and F.-J. Sladeczek (Munich,
2002).

[7] See, for example, H. Belting, *Likeness and Presence: A History of the Image before
the Era of Art*, trans. E. Jephcott (Chicago, 1994); and L. Dupré, *Passage to Modernity:
An Essay in the Hermeneutics of Nature and Culture* (New Haven, 1993). Compare the
account of the Lutheran treatment of religious works in J. L. Koerner, *The Reformation
of the Image* (Chicago, 2004). On new sanctuaries and pilgrimage sites, many of them
created about paintings or statues, see L. Rothkrug, "Popular Religion and Holy
Shrines," in *Religion and the People, 800–1700*, ed. J. Obelkevich (Chapel Hill, 1979),
20–86; idem, *Religious Practices and Collective Perceptions: Hidden Homologies in the
Renaissance and Reformation*, published as a monograph in *Historical Reflections/Reflex-
ions historiques*, 7:1 (1980), noting also S. D. Sargent, "A Critique of Lionel Rothkrug's
List of Bavarian Pilgrimage Shrines," *Archiv für Reformationsgeschichte*, 78 (1987), 358;
and the preliminary Italian data offered in *Per una storia dei santuari cristiani d'Italia:
approcci regionali*, ed. G. Cracco (Bologna, 2002).

that is unusual about this case, from Rinaldeschi's execution to the miraculous qualities of the painting he offended, was conditioned by a heightened anxiety over religious images in post-Savonarolan Florence. Yet our chief goal in this study has not been to generalize from the Florentine to other historical situations, but rather to test the sources concerning Rinaldeschi to see whether they might reveal more about the specific circumstances that led to his death and about the Florence in which he lived and died. inferiority inferiority inferiority inferiority

This project had its beginning during a discussion over a lunch at the Institute for Advanced Study in Princeton in the course of which Connell told Constable about a curious story in manuscript he had come across in the Bancroft Library in Berkeley, and Constable told Connell about a curious painting of a similar subject he had come across in the storeroom of the Stibbert Museum in Florence. Although both authors have made contributions throughout, Connell, as a historian of Florence and Renaissance Italy, has been primarily responsible for Chapters 1 and 3, and Constable, as a historian of the Middle Ages, has been primarily responsible for Chapter 2.

Among the friends and colleagues who helped with this essay, which touches on many topics, special thanks are owing, in addition to those mentioned in specific notes, to Candace Adelson, Kirsten Aschengreen Piacenti (for permission to publish the colour photographs of the Stibbert picture), the late Elizabeth Beatson, Amy Bloch, Dwayne Carpenter, Olivia Constable, Gino Corti (for checking several transcriptions), Gregory Hanlon, Rab Hatfield, Richard Jackson, Jennifer Jamer (for help with the index), Christiane Klapisch-Zuber, Irving and Marilyn Lavin (for helpful observations on the picture), Hubert Mordek, John Najemy, Michael Rocke (for obtaining photographs of the record of Rinaldeschi's trial before the Eight for Security), Frederick Russell, the Scolopi Fathers in Florence (for permission to consult their archive), Nikki Shepardson, and Patricia Woolf (for the title and other suggestions). We are also grateful to the editors of the *Journal of the Warburg and Courtauld Studies* for permission to republish work that appeared previously in print, and especially to Konrad Eisenbichler and to the anonymous readers of the Centre for Reformation and Renaissance Studies for their helpful suggestions.

A Note on Chronology

Florence in the Renaissance followed the Julian calendar consisting of twelve months and 365 days, with a leap year every four years. However, as in many other parts of Europe, Florence began the year on 25 March, the Feast of the Annunciation. Thus Florentine documents that date from 1 January to 24 March do not give the number of the year that would appear in modern style, but rather of the previous year. In this study all years are numbered according to modern style, save in the transcriptions of documents, where, if a year does not agree with modern style, both styles are given. For instance, where a document reads "10 January 1497," which according to modern style was 1498, this is written as "10 January 1497/8."

A second system for numbering years, the indiction system, was also used in Renaissance Florence, as in much of Europe, in order to ensure greater accuracy when dating official documents. According to this system each year was numbered progressively from 1 until 15, at which point the numbering began again from 1. Florence followed what is known as the Caesarean system of indictions, in which the indiction year began on 24 September. Thus the date of Rinaldeschi's arrest and trial, 21 July 1501, fell in the fourth indiction year, and the fifth indiction year began little more than two months later, on 24 September 1501.

For indications of the time of day, see p. 27 below.

A NOTE ON CURRENCY

Two systems of metal coinage were in use in Renaissance Florence. Gold florins were used by merchants, especially in international trade; while silver and copper-based coins, known as *monete di piccioli*, translated here as "common coinage," were used for most local transactions. Common coinage transactions were recorded in units known as the lira, the soldo and the denaro, the lira being worth 20 soldi, and the soldo worth 12 denari.

About the year 1500 the gold florin converted to common coinage at a rate of approximately 7 lire. The gold florins that circulated in Rinaldeschi's Florence, described as *fiorini larghi di oro in oro* and here translated as "broad gold florins," were introduced in 1471. The average daily wage for an unskilled laborer was about 9 soldi. In the sixteenth century another gold coin, the ducat, became more common. It was roughly equivalent with the florin and it, too, could be converted to approximately 7 lire in common coinage.

CHAPTER 1
THE CULPRIT AND HIS OFFENCES

In the summer of 1501, on 11 July, in the city of Florence, a citizen called Antonio Rinaldeschi lost some money and clothing while gambling at a tavern called "The Fig Tree." Leaving the tavern, he cursed the name of the Virgin. Then, while crossing a small piazza in front of the church of S. Maria degli Alberighi, he stooped to gather a handful of dry horse dung. Above a doorway on a side wall of the church, in a small alley off the piazza, stood a tabernacle with a painted fresco of the Virgin Annunciate, known as the Madonna or S. Maria de' Ricci. Rinaldeschi threw his handful of dung at the face of this Virgin. Then he fled to a villa outside the city and apparently remained at large for several days.

It is possible Rinaldeschi thought that the dry dung would fall to the ground and his crime remain undetected. But a portion of it, resembling a rosette of plaster or gesso, ("quasi pareva una rosetta secha"), stuck to the Virgin's diadem or crown, above the nape of her neck. The dirtied image drew much attention. The archbishop came to look. Candles and votive images were brought before the fresco, which quickly became an object of popular devotion.

The committee of magistrates known as the Eight for Security undertook the task of finding the culprit. A boy who had witnessed the crime said it was done by a grown man. Perhaps it was after inquiring at the Fig Tree that the Eight came to suspect Rinaldeschi of committing the crime. All who knew him were asked to come forward, and several days later he was found—some said by a miracle—in the garden of the Franciscan convent of S. Francesco al Monte alle Croci, above Florence. When he realized he was taken, Rinaldeschi tried to commit suicide, thrusting a dagger into his breast. But the blade struck a rib, sparing his life. The wounded prisoner was conducted to Florence for imprisonment, apparently in the Palace of the Podestà or Bargello, where he was examined by the Eight on 21 July, probably in the evening.

Before the magistrates, the arrested man confessed and, according to one source, asked to be executed in order to avoid being lynched by the people. He was sentenced to be hanged from the windows of the Bargello and not at the usual place of execution outside the city because the crowd would have interfered with the procession. Rinaldeschi's possessions were confiscated by the Eight. The criminal confessed to a priest and received absolution, and later that night the hooded members of the Company of the Blacks (*Compagnia dei Neri*), the confraternity that accompanied condemned criminals to their executions, escorted him to the window of the palace, and he was hanged. His body hung outside the palace during the morning of the following day, which on this account was described in one source as "a double feast," because 22 July was the feast of St. Mary Magdalene, which was celebrated in Florence with processions, bell-ringing, and a horse-race, all sponsored by the Podestà. The same morning, now that the evidence of the crime was no longer needed, the vicar of the archbishop had the offended image cleaned, although it is not clear how thorough a job was done, as the "rosette" of dung apparently remained, or else returned as a sign (*segno*) of the incident. Later in the day Rinaldeschi's body was taken down and buried.

The foregoing narrative has been constructed from several sources. The original sentence pronounced against Rinaldeschi by the Eight for Security and that described his actions is preserved in the Florentine State Archive [Figure 11].[1] The writer's hand is rushed, which probably reflects the urgency with which the Eight proclaimed their sentence in the middle of the night. The sentence is supplemented by an official record of Rinaldeschi's execution, which is interesting chiefly for the scribe's departure from the ordinary way of registering the execution of a sentence. A condemned person's fulfillment of the terms of his or her sentence was usually indicated by the appearance of the word *paghò* or "he paid" in the register's margin. Next to Rinaldeschi's name, however, the scribe wrote "paghò contanti" – "he paid in cash" – which was a brief way of stating his opinion that Rinaldeschi got what he deserved.[2]

---

[1] ASF, OGB, 120, fol. 128[r–v], transcribed in the Appendix as Document I.

[2] ASF, OGB, 229, "Libro delle condanne," fol. 10v: "Antonio di Giovanni Rinaldeschi, addì 22 di luglio 1501 fu condannato che sia impichato alla finestra del Podestà, al libro 120, a carte 128. Finestra et forche." [Antonio ... was condemned to be hanged from the window of the Podestà, in book no. 120, page 128. Window and hanging.] On the marginal notation, "he paid in cash," compare Charles Dickens, *Martin Chuzzlewit*, chapter 51, on Jonas Chuzzlewit of Montague Tigg (a.k.a. Tigg Montague), when he was murdered: "He has given his receipt in full—or had it forced from him rather."

An account of the crime and execution is included in the so-called San Miniato codex, which consists of records kept by the Company of the Blacks of those condemned to death in Florence from 1423 until 1759,[3] and the hanging and burial were also recorded in at least two different versions in other registers kept by the Company of the Blacks.[4]

---

[3]This nineteenth-century manuscript, according to its owner (in 1901) and editor, Giuseppe Rondini, is "perhaps a copy of an earlier manuscript belonging to the Company of St. Urban," which was associated with the Confraternity of S. Giovanni Decollato in San Miniato (hence Rondini's name "Codice Sanminiatese") in assisting those condemned to death and affiliated with the Florentine Company of the Blacks. The records were published in G. Rondini "I 'giustiziati' a Firenze (dal secolo XV al secolo XVIII)," *Archivio storico italiano*, 5th ser., 28 (1901), 209–256, esp. 209 n. 2 on the manuscript, 222 n. 2 on other sources, and 225–226 on Rinaldeschi. The report seems to be related to the inscriptions on the Stibbert picture discussed in the article, to which Rondini refers, but it includes some details (such as that Rinaldeschi was found by a miracle of the Virgin and was executed at one o'clock at night) not found in other sources. Rondini also stated that the case of Rinaldeschi was published ("fu data alla stampa"), perhaps referring to the earliest of the fliers we have seen, a *Relazione della miracolosa immagine della SS. Annunziata, che si venera nella Chiesa della Madonna de' Ricci de' Cherici Regolari delle Scuole Pie* (Florence, 1718), now reprinted in R. Tassi, *Chiesa Madonna de' Ricci (dedicata alla Vergine Annunziata). Dal Giubileo di Bonifacio VIII e di Dante al Giubileo d'inizio del Terzo millennio* (Florence, 1998), 365–368, which conflates several contemporary sources. A. Zorzi, "Le esecuzioni delle condanne a morte a Firenze nel tardo medioevo tra repressione penale e cerimoniale pubblico," in *Simbolo e realtà della vita urbana nel tardo medioevo*, ed. M. Miglio and G. Lombardi (Viterbo, 1993), 51–58, gives (in a separately paginated offprint at 6 n. 21) the current location of the San Miniato codex as Florence, Biblioteca Riccardiana Moreniana, MS Palagi, 174.

[4]See the Appendix, Documents III and IV. Document III was published with some variations in G. Richa, *Notizie istoriche delle chiese fiorentine* (Florence, 1754–1762), II, 133; C. Torricelli, *La chiesa della Madonna de' Ricci in Firenze. Note storiche e artistiche*, 2nd ed., ed. L. Stefani (Florence, 1980), 13; and S. Y. Edgerton, Jr., *Pictures and Punishment: Art and Criminal Prosecution during the Florentine Renaissance* (Ithaca, 1985), 55 n. 40. Document IV was copied in 1637 from a book that belonged to the Company of the Blacks. (The copy is in APTPS, Reg. Dom., 505, S.M.R., 15, "Documenti relativi a S. Maria de' Ricci dalle origini," fol. 4r–v). An untranscribed photograph of a later and somewhat inaccurate copy of the 1637 copy is published in Tassi, *Chiesa Madonna de' Ricci* (n. 3 above), 373. On the Company of the Blacks, a "sub-group" of the Company of S. Maria della Croce al Tempio which existed from 1423 to 1785, see F. Fineschi, "La rappresentazione della morte sul patibolo nella liturgia fiorentina della congregazione dei Neri," *Archivio storico italiano*, 150 (1992), 805–846; Zorzi, "Le esecuzioni" (n. 3 above), 51–58; and K. Eisenbichler, "Lorenzo de' Medici and the Confraternity of

Yet another description of Rinaldeschi's actions and his punishment appears in an account book that was kept by one Giovanni Landi for an association, or *opera*, formed by the rector and prominent members of the parish of S. Maria degli Alberighi to foster devotion to the damaged fresco.[5] The book of the *opera* was begun on 26 July 1501, only four days after Rinaldeschi's hanging, and it provides remarkable testimony of the speed with which the parishioners moved to take advantage of the episode. The register, now owned by the Bancroft Library of the University of California at Berkeley, contains records that continue until 1542, albeit with some chronological intervals. In addition, passages from two other account books once belonging to the same *opera*, but whose whereabouts are now unknown, were published by the eighteenth-century antiquarian Giuseppe Richa.[6]

Further descriptions of the Rinaldeschi affair include a passage dated 21 July 1501 that was copied in 1630 from a family record book or *priorista* that in 1630 belonged to Matteo Segaloni. This adds the detail, not confirmed elsewhere, that Rinaldeschi was unable to flee farther from the city because he was suffering the painful symptoms of syphilis.[7] The affair of Rinaldeschi is also described in the *Diary* of Luca

---

the Blacks in Florence," *Fides et Historia*, 26 (1994), 85–98 (88–90). Note that Zorzi (n. 3 above), 5–7 (offprint), counts at least 20 surviving manuscripts with lists of Florentine *giustiziati*, all of them derived from the records of the Blacks.

[5] Bancroft Library, University of California, Berkeley, Banc., MSS, 54. The book passed from German hands to the collection of Henry R. Hatfield, where it was described in S. De Ricci and W. J. Wilson, *Census of Medieval and Renaissance Manuscripts in the United States and Canada*, 3 vols. (New York, 1935–1940), I,10. It was acquired by the University of California *circa* 1950; cf. C.U. Faye and W.H. Bond, *Supplement to the Census of Medieval and Renaissance Manuscripts in the United States and Canada* (New York, 1962), 2. We are grateful to Anthony Bliss of the Bancroft Library for his help. The description of Rinaldeschi's deed appears in the Appendix as Document II.

[6] These two other registers—each belonging to the *opera*'s system of accounts – were cited by Richa, *Notizie* (n. 4 above), VIII, 237 ("Lib. segnato 'A,' intitolato 'Entrata, e Uscita dell'Oratorio . . . dal 1501 al 1540,'" from which he quoted fol. 140), and at VIII, 249–250 ("Libro di Ricordi scripto dal 1508 al 1540"). The passage quoted from the second of these registers, at VIII, 249–250, was clearly derived from the "Narration" that appears in the earlier Berkeley register on fol. 131^r, where an unidentified sixteenth-century writer stated (at the bottom of the folio) that it contained the earliest record (*primo richordo*) of Rinaldeschi's crime.

[7] APTPS, Reg. Dom., 505, S.M.R., 15, fol. 5^{r-v}, in the Appendix as Document VII. The *priorista* from which this notice was copied is possibly ASF, Manoscritti, 226, described in the inventory as the "Priorista fiorentino" of one Francesco Segaloni,

Landucci, from which it was later copied, with a few differences, by Agostino Lapini in his later diary, and Carlo Strozzi, who compiled a manuscript with records concerning Florentine churches, monasteries, hospitals and confraternities. According to Landucci's account, after a boy witnessed the crime, the culprit was "tailed" (*codiato*) and arrested on the very same day.[8]

The most unusual of the sources regarding this episode, however, is certainly a painting, now in the Stibbert Museum in Florence, which depicts the events leading to Rinaldeschi's death across nine separate panels, each accompanied by an inscription [Figures 1–10].[9] This remarkable painting needs to be understood not in the tradition of *pitture infamanti*—public and quasi-official paintings and portraits of notorious criminals [Figure 12][10]— but, as we shall see, as the record of a *cause célèbre* which gave rise to a popular devotion. The last panel shows in the centre not Rinaldeschi's body but the battle for his soul between the angels and devils and is inscribed "My Lord Jesus Christ have mercy on my soul" [Figure 9].[11] This, and the date 21 July 1501 in the first panel [Figure 1], are the only original inscriptions. Others were added in the late sixteenth or seventeenth century, probably as memory faded and some written record of the events was needed.[12] The painting, with its almost comic-strip character—which was unusual but not unprecedented at that

---

presumably a relative. Matteo Segaloni was an architect active at Florence in the first half of the seventeenth century.

[8] Luca Landucci, *Diario fiorentino dal 1450 al 1516*, ed. I. Del Badia (Florence, 1883), 233–234. The translation by A. de Rosen Jervis (London-New York, 1927) is unreliable. See also Agostino Lapini, *Diario fiorentino dal 252 al 1596*, ed. G. O. Corazzini (Florence, 1900), 44; and Carlo Strozzi, "Raccolta di memorie, fondazioni e padronati di diverse chiese, monasteri, spedali, compagnie e simili," in ASF, Carte strozziane, ser. III, 233, fol. 130v. The passage from Landucci's *Diary* appears with a fresh translation in the Appendix as Document V. The account in Strozzi's miscellany, which is cited in Eckstein, "Words and Deeds" (above, Foreword n. 3), 16 n.61, is published in the Appendix as Document VI.

[9] On this painting see *Il Museo Stibbert*, ed. L. G. Boccia, G. Cantelli and F. Maraini, IV:1 (Florence, 1976), 32. Its accession number is 16719.

[10] G. Ortalli, ". . . *pingatur in Palatio* . . .": *La pittura infamante nei secoli XIII–XVI* (Rome, 1979); and Edgerton, *Pictures* (n. 4 above), 71–73. The engraving in Figure 12 shows one of these images being painted on the Palace of the Podestà.

[11] See Edgerton, *Pictures* (n. 4 above), 58: "The real subject of the panel . . . is not the hanging of Rinaldeschi but rather his redemption."

[12] See below, pp. 24–25 on the date.

time[13]—has attracted considerable attention in recent years, even in the popular press.[14] It is sometimes noted for its careful portrayal of such aspects of daily life as the tavern's kitchen—and indeed there was a tavern called "The Fig Tree" located in the vicinity of the church[15]—, and for its representations of buildings and streets. Iodoco del Badia, in his 1883 edition of Landucci's *Diary*, presumably referred to the Stibbert painting when he said that the memory of the Rinaldeschi incident "has been preserved until modern times, an ancient picture representing the fact being exhibited under the portico of the church of the Madonna de' Ricci every year on this day."[16]

---

[13]Compare the predella with six scenes of the profanation of the host by Paolo Uccello (1467–1468) in the Galleria Nazionale delle Marche, Urbino, on which see J. Pope-Hennessy, *Paolo Uccello*, 2nd ed. (London, 1969),156–157, figs. 87–92; and the cycle of episodes from the life of St. Francesca Romana attributed to Antoniazzo Romano in the monastery of Tor de' Specchi in Rome, on which see G. Kaftal, *Iconography of the Saints in Central and South Italian Schools of Painting* (Florence, 1965), cols. 447–451, no.154. See generally D. Kunzle, *The Early Comic Strip: Narrative Strips and Picture Stories in European Broadsheets from c. 1450 to 1825* (Berkeley – Los Angeles, 1973), esp. 26–27.

[14]See the exhibition catalogue by L. Collobi Ragghianti, *La casa italiana nei secoli* (Florence, 1948), 35, cited in *Il Museo Stibbert* (n. 9 above), IV:1, 32; C. Ragghianti, "Fumetti del Rinascimento," *Sele arte*, 1:5 (1953), 62–63; *La Nazione* (12 September 1984), 3; D. Gontard, "Santa Maria del Sacrilegio," *FMR*, Italian edition, 17:9 (1991), 117–132; G. Magherini and V. Biotti, *L'Isola delle Stinche e i percorsi della follia a Firenze nei secoli XIV–XVIII* (Florence, 1992), figs. 15–17; the entry by L. Burkart in *Iconoclasme: vie et mort de l'image médiévale* (Paris 2001), 112; and the entry by N. Pons in *Firenze: alle origini dello "stile fiorentino"* (Tokyo, 2005), 90–91. There are also mentions in R. Trexler, *Public Life in Renaissance Florence* (New York, 1980), 22; and M. Boskovits, *Immagini da meditare. Ricerche su dipinti di tema religioso nei secoli XII–XV* (Milan, 1994), 77 n.12.

[15]BNCF, Nuovi acquisti, 987, which is a description of the city's four quarters from the 1520s, contains the following entry at fol. 133v: "L'hostaria del Fico. Fàlla Giovanni et El Moretto. Tengono garzoni otto, et alla cucina stàvi quattro garzoni." [The tavern of The Fig Tree. Giovanni and El Moretto run it. They keep eight apprentices and in the kitchen there are four apprentices.] We are grateful to Elizabeth Pilliod for this reference.

[16]Landucci, *Diario* (n. 8 above), 233–234: "si è conservata la memoria fino ai moderni tempi, esponendosi tutti gli anni in quel giorno, sotto le loggie della Chiesa della Madonna de' Ricci, un'antica tavola rappresentante il fatto." Tassi, *Chiesa Madonna de' Ricci* (n. 3 above), 127, states that the painting was sold in the late eighteenth century, but Del Badia's comment suggests that the sale took place after 1883.

The painting tells a story, but in a special way, since in the three scenes of the upper tier the action moves from right to left, against the direction of the panels, whereas in the middle and lower tiers it moves left to right, with the panels. This change corresponds to a shift in the attitude towards Rinaldeschi, who is depicted as a bad man, tempted by devils, in the upper panels and with greater sympathy in the middle and lower panels, where the devils are expelled and replaced by angels. It is as if the first tier shows Rinaldeschi's sin, the second his redemption, and the third his salvation.

A progression from crime to salvation is intrinsic to the tradition concerning the "Good Thief": of the two thieves who were crucified with Christ, this one repented and was rewarded with salvation. Representations of the Good Thief became common in the later middle ages, and the Stibbert picture—especially the last scene, with the appeal that appears to ensure Rinaldeschi's salvation—was influenced by this tradition in its telling of the Rinaldeschi story.[17] But the painter drew on other models as well. Some of the panels resemble scenes from the lives of Christ and of the saints, such as St. Peter in Prison [Figures 6 and 13].[18] The Christological parallels include not only Rinaldeschi's arrest in the garden [Figures 4 and 14][19] and bleeding wound, which reappears (perhaps miraculously) in the final scene [Figures 4 and 9], but also the rope he carries [Figure 8], presumably that with which he is hanged in the following scene, where the battle between the angels and devils looks like part of a Last Judgment [Figure 9]. Among other features of the painting, which abounds in iconographical topoi, are the contemplative pose (resembling some personifications of philosophy) of the right-hand gambler, who may be wearing Rinaldeschi's forfeited cloak [Figure 1]; the painting on the wall behind him with a snake and a woman holding a tree that represents the Original Sin; the reversal of the crossed swords of the coat-of-arms on the shield [Figure 4] and those held by the angels

---

[17] On the tradition of the Good Thief see Mitchell B. Merback, *The Thief, the Cross and the Wheel: Pain and the Spectacle of Punishment in Medieval and Renaissance Europe* (Chicago,1999), 22–27, and throughout.

[18] For Filippino Lippi's fresco of *St Paul Visiting St. Peter in Prison* see U. Baldini, *The Brancacci Chapel Frescoes* (New York, 1992), 182.

[19] For Duccio's *Christ Taken Prisoner* see F. Deuchler, *Duccio* (Milan, 1984), 211–212 and also 87–88, figs. 98, 100. See also A. Derbes, *Picturing the Passion in Late Medieval Italy: Narrative Painting, Franciscan Ideologies, and the Levant* (New York, 1996), 35–71, on "The Betrayal of Christ."

[Figure 9]; Rinaldeschi's curious hat [Figure 5], which looks like a black version of the red hat worn by one of the soldiers; and the angel escorting one of the Company of the Blacks [Figure 8].

The painting has been most recently attributed to the workshop of the painter Bartolommeo di Giovanni.[20] With the discovery of the Berkeley register, however, there are reasons for ascribing it to Filippo di Lorenzo Dolciati, to whom several payments were made for work done in 1502, when an oratory was built to enclose the fresco of the Virgin. The oratory was called S. Maria de' Ricci or Madonna de' Ricci, after the image Rinaldeschi profaned. The image was originally situated in a tabernacle commissioned by Rosso de' Ricci for the much older church of S. Maria degli Alberighi [Figure 22] and the street corner became known as the "canto de' Ricci."[21] With the rapid building of an oratory, the *opera* sought to provide a proper home for the new devotion to the Madonna. The painter of the project, Filippo Dolciati, received 12 lire common coinage on 24 February 1502 for painting and colours for the ceiling and three Prophets, and on 24 March he received 7 lire for a predella above the altar, a Pietà on the altar's face, and various embellishments such as azure and gold stars for the ceiling, as well as seven lire, seven soldi as reimbursement for supplies.[22] It seems likely that the predella was none other than the Stibbert painting, which, although taller than most predellas, needed to fill an unusually large space between the altar and the Madonna above the door.[23] It is not clear when precisely the Stibbert painting was separated from its possible original position beneath the Madonna de' Ricci, but probably this took place as a consequence of the series of subsequent building campaigns in which the oratory of the Madonna completely absorbed the neighbouring church of S. Maria degli Alberighi. In addition, although this was not specified by the account book, Dolciati was almost certainly employed to repaint the Madonna herself, as the records of a court case from 1545 make clear.[24] Thus the date "21 July

---

[20] Ragghianti, "Fumetti" (n.14 above), 62.

[21] On the church, see below p. 62 n. 39).

[22] Banc., MSS, 54, fols. 21^r (24 February 1501/2) and 23^r (24 March 1501/2), published in the Appendix as Document VIII.

[23] The Stibbert panel's dimensions are 102 X 115.5 cm.

[24] See below, pp. 66–68, and Figures 26 and 27. The face of the Angel, in particular, bears some resemblance to faces in the Stibbert painting.

1501," which appears on the panel, refers to the event, not the painting, which should now be dated 1502.

The painter of the Stibbert panel was not an important artist. So far it has not been possible to identify securely other surviving works of Filippo Dolciati. About his career we know very little, save that he was born in 1443, that he was the son of a painter, that he enrolled in the Company of Saint Luke in 1460, and that he died in 1519.[25] It seems likely that Dolciati was one of the many trade painters in Florence called *madonnieri*, who specialized in devotional images. He seems to have had a family association with the parish of S. Maria degli Alberighi, since the Dolciati owned one of the houses that were destroyed to make place for the oratory,[26] and since the records of the Madonna de' Ricci mention a funeral monument bearing the name of Dolciati (dated 1533).[27]

The surviving accounts of the crime tell much the same story. It is possible that the scribe who recorded the official sentence, which was contemporary with the event, heard the testimony of the parish priest or other parishioners, since the two versions, the Latin sentence of the Eight and the vernacular narrative in the account book, are quite similar. Most convincing is the fact that where the account book states of the horse dung that "a bit of it remained stuck in the diadem" (*rimase un pocho apichata nella* [sic] *diadema*) the Eight's register states that "part of said dung, as is said in the vernacular, 'remained stuck in the diadem'" (*parte dicti sterchoris, ut vulgariter dicitur, 'rimase apichato nella* [sic] *diadema'*).

Only in a few details do the several accounts disagree. Although the sentence of the Eight, the account book, and the painting agree in calling the criminal "Antonio," Landucci called him "Rinaldo," a

---

[25] D. E. Colnaghi, *Dictionary of Florentine Painters from the 13th to the 17th Centuries*, 2nd ed., ed. C. Malvani (Florence, 1986), 89. ASF, Accademia del Disegno, 1, fol. 8[v], records the entry into the Company of Saint Luke in 1460 of "Filippo di Lorenzo di Filippo Dolciati dipintore." [Filippo the son of Lorenzo the son of Filippo Dolciati, painter.]

[26] Richa, *Notizie* (n. 4 above), VIII, 237.

[27] ASF, Manoscritti, 628, "Sepoltuario", 51 (Chiesa della Madonna de' Ricci, anno 1609): "Tondo in marmo con suo chiusino e tassel' simile anesso col d.to monumento. Simone di Piero di Lorenzo Dolciati e *suorum*, 1533." [Tondo in marble with its cover and similar inlay attached to said monument. Simone the son of Piero the son of Lorenzo Dolciati and his relations, 1533.]

shortened form of the family name "Rinaldeschi" that reflects Landucci's gathering of the news of the day as it circulated in Florentine
streets. Another discrepancy concerns the name of Antonio's father,
whom the records of the Eight called "Giovanni" ("Antonius Iohannis") whereas on the painting he is named "Giuseppe." But the
inscriptions on the panels were probably added later, and there is little
reason to credit them in this particular. Rinaldeschi appears as the son
of Giovanni everywhere else, and a scribal error is unlikely. Indeed,
"Giuseppe" was rare as a baptismal name in fifteenth-century Florence,
probably owing to the ambivalence that surrounded St. Joseph in the
popular tradition that saw him as God's cuckold.[28]

With one exception, the sources agree that Rinaldeschi was tried
and hanged in the Palace of the Podestà. One of the accounts deriving
from the records of the Blacks, preserved in a seventeenth-century copy,
instead states that Rinaldeschi was "tried in the Temple," that he asked
to be hanged there, and that he was also "buried at the Temple." In
contemporary documents "the Temple" referred variously to one of
two churches, both associated with the confraternity of the Blacks. The
church of S. Maria della Croce al Tempio, which was where the Blacks
held their regular meetings, was located at the beginning of the Via
de' Malcontenti, along the procession route that was followed by
prisoners being led to the scaffold—hence the name "Via de' Malcontenti."[29] Also referred to as "The Temple" was an oratory in a cemetery
maintained by the Blacks beyond the city walls, near the scaffold, where
the condemned could receive last rites and a Christian burial [Figure
15].[30] Although an error in transcription possibly led the writer of this
account to place Rinaldeschi's sentencing and execution "in the Temple," the account is probably correct in offering the detail not attested

---

[28] On St. Joseph see C. Klapisch-Zuber, "Zacharie, ou Le père évincé. Les rites
nuptiaux toscans entre Giotto et le Concile de Trente," in her *La maison et le nom.
Stratégies et rituels dans l'Italie de la Renaissance* (Paris, 1990), 151–183, esp. 166–180,
where it is noted that Joseph's feast day was not celebrated in Florence until 1508;
and Carolyn C. Wilson, *St. Joseph in Italian Renaissance Society and Art: New Directions
and Interpretations* (Philadelphia, 2001). D. Herlihy, "Tuscan Names, 1200–1530,"
Renaissance Quarterly, 41 (1988), 561–582, does not mention "Giuseppe."

[29] Eisenbichler, "Lorenzo de' Medici" (n. 4 above), 89 n. 21.

[30] F. Fineschi, *Cristo e Giuda: rituali di giustizia a Firenze in età moderna* (Florence,
1995), 41, gives a detail from a map of Florence circa 1470, the *Mappa della Catena*,
that labels this chapel as "Il Tempio."

elsewhere that Rinaldeschi was buried "at the Temple," meaning the cemetery and oratory outside the city. This is seconded in part by the inscription on the last panel of the Stibbert painting, which states that Rinaldeschi was "buried," and the cemetery of the Blacks would have been the appropriate place.

More difficult to reconcile are a statement in the account book that Rinaldeschi's deed was unseen, and Landucci's remark that a child had seen a man commit the crime and that he was followed and watched. It is not clear from the surviving accounts how Rinaldeschi came to be suspected of the crime. Some of the accounts suggest that Rinaldeschi was arrested on the very day he committed his crime, but the one that is closest to the event, the parish record preserved in the Bancroft manuscript, states quite clearly that there was a ten-day period between Rinaldeschi's deed and his arrest. Although it is possible that a child turned Rinaldeschi in, it is also easy to imagine that agents of the Eight, through inquiries made in the neighbourhood, discovered that Rinaldeschi's gambling losses at the nearby Fig Tree had occurred about the time of the crime. The account in the San Miniato codex says that Rinaldeschi was discovered by a miracle of the Virgin.

Finally, there are some discrepancies regarding the time of Rinaldeschi's execution. The Eight for Security simply decreed that he should hang until the fourteenth hour of the following day, and in the records of S. Maria degli Alberighi, where the hour of execution is left blank, Rinaldeschi is said to have been left hanging until the following morning. He was hanged "at the hour of one at night" in the San Miniato codex and in one of the records kept by the Blacks, "at the second hour of the night of 21 July" in another of the records of the Blacks, simply "at night" in Landucci's diary, and at "the seventh hour of the night" on the Stibbert painting, which shows a man holding a flare from a window above the body and further says that he was condemned "at the twenty-fourth hour of the night." In fifteenth-century Italy the day was commonly divided into twenty-four equal hours beginning half-an-hour after sunset and sometimes divided into two sets of twelve day-time and twelve night-time hours.[31] Remem-

---

[31] See F. Lehner, *Die mittelalterliche Tageseinteilung in den österreichischen Ländern*, Quellenstudien aus dem historischen Seminar der Universität Innsbruck 3 (Innsbruck, 1911), 60–105, esp. 70; and H. Grotefend, *Taschenbuch der Zeitrechnung des deutschen Mittelalters und der Neuzeit*, 8th–9th ed. (Hanover-Leipzig, 1948), 24. See K. M.

bering that the inscriptions on the Stibbert painting are probably a later addition, it seems probable that Rinaldeschi was tried late in the day of 21 July and hanged that night, by modern reckoning at either eleven o'clock or perhaps four o'clock, and that he remained hanging until eleven o'clock of the morning of 22 July.[32]

Very little is told about Rinaldeschi himself in the immediate sources except that on the painting he is described as a "nobleman." His putative ancestors belonged to a prominent magnate family of the subject town of Prato.[33] In the second half of the fourteenth century some family members moved to Florence, where they established a funeral monument in S. Maria Novella and one branch changed its name to the more plebeian "Naldini."[34] An Antonio Rinaldeschi, possibly the grandson or

---

Setton, *The Papacy and the Levant (1204–1571)*, III (Philadelphia, 1984), 7 n. 36, on the time of the death of Pius III in 1503. See also M. Quinlan-McGrath, "The Astrological Vault of the Villa Farnesina: Agostino Chigi's Rising Sign," *Journal of the Warburg and Courtauld Institutes*, 47 (1984), 91–105 (100); and I. D. Rowland, "The Birth Date of Agostino Chigi: Documentary Proof," ibid., 192–193 (193).

[32] This also agrees with the inscription of 21 July 1501 on the first panel of the Stibbert painting, which is almost certainly contemporary with the painting and which records the date of Rinaldeschi's death.

[33] S. Raveggi, "Protagonisti e antagonisti nel libero Comune," in F. Braudel, *Prato. Storia di una città*, 4 vols. (Florence, 1991–1997), I, *Ascesa e declino del centro medievale*, ed. G. Cherubini, part 2, 613–736 (709 n. 171), discusses the family's fortunes in the first half of the fourteenth century and mentions a "Giovanni di Arrigaccio." On the various social meanings of magnate lineage in the postcommunal period see C. Donati, *L'idea di nobiltà in Italia, secoli XIV–XVII* (Rome-Bari, 1988); and C. Klapisch-Zuber, "Ruptures de parenté et changements d'identité chez les magnats florentins du XIVe siècle," *Annales, E.S.C.*, 43 (1988), 1205–1240.

[34] We are indebted for information on the Rinaldeschi family to Christiane Klapisch-Zuber (who consulted the analyses of the Florentine catasti compiled by herself and David Herlihy) and Anthony Molho (who consulted the 1480 catasto and the records of the Monte delle doti). The only Rinaldeschi who appears among the citizens eligible for public office in the Florentine catasto of 1427 was Rinaldo di Dego (ASF, Catasto, 77, fol. 324[v]), who was born in 1397, and whose cousin Francesco di Domenico (ASF, Catasto, 80, fol. 124[r–v])—together with his descendants, down to 1517—appears instead under the name "Naldini." The change of name was probably to permit members of the family to follow business careers and qualify for public office as *populares*, and this is confirmed by the "Priorista Mariani," ASF, Manoscritti, 252, V, fols. 1191[r] (Naldini) and 1199[v]–1200[r] (Rinaldeschi), which documents several of the Rinaldeschi moving from Prato to Florence in the fourteenth century. The question is complicated, however, by the existence of an (apparently) unrelated family named Naldini, mentioned in E. Fiumi, *Volterra e San Gimignano nel medioevo*, ed. G. Pinto (San Gimignano, 1983), 226. Two men named Rinaldeschi

nephew of a Giovanni, lived in Bologna about 1400, and these may have been the direct ancestors of our Antonio, whose father, Giovanni, had certainly settled in Florence before 1481.[35]

We know from Giovanni's will, which was drawn up 5 December 1499 in the infirmary of the Badia Fiorentina, a Benedictine abbey in the heart of Florence, that this branch of the Rinaldeschi owned a house in the Via dell'Alloro as well as a tomb in the church of S. Maria Maggiore. Our Antonio, who must have been at least thirty years old at the time he committed his crime, was Giovanni's son by his first wife Alessandra, and he had several half-sisters by his father's later wives, Bartolommea and Angela. His debts were the cause of a quarrel with his father, who pronounced him an "unworthy heir" (heredi inmerito) in his will.[36] After his father's death, on 29 March 1500,[37] Antonio

---

appear in the 1480 catasto—Bartholomeo di Giovanni di Bindo (ASF, Catasto-Campione del Monte, 101, fol. 314[r]) and Biagio di Giovanni di Biagio (ibid., 101, fol. 225[r])—but their relation, if any, to our Antonio di Giovanni di Antonio is not known. According to the "Priorista Mariani," V, fol. 1191[r], "Per esser stata poco numerosa in questo ramo, che venne in Firenze, si vedono in essa pochi godimenti di antichi magistrati." [Since the members of this branch that came to Florence were few, the family held few old magistracies.]

[35] See ASF, Carte del Bene, 49, in which Letters 139 (dated 1381–1382) and 224 (recommending a "nipote") were written by a Giovanni Rinaldeschi; and Letters 297, 301, 304, 315, 319, and 320 (all undated but possibly from circa 1410) were written by an Antonio Rinaldeschi then in Bologna.

[36] ASF, NA, 16795, Ser Piero di Andrea da Campi, no. 165, fols. 431[r]–432[r] (432[r]). Since another source (Appendix, Doc. IV) called Antonio a "battitore di padre" [beater of his father], and the testament stated no other reason for Giovanni's being in the infirmary when it was written, it is possible the testament was drawn up after a confrontation between father and son. A daughter, Lucrezia, by a later wife, was baptized in Florence on 1 May 1481 (Florence, Archivio dell'Opera di S. Maria del Fiore, Battesimi maschi [sic], fol. 124[v]: "Lucretia et Iacopa di Giovanni de Antonio Rinaldeschi nacque a dì primo, hore 15" [Lucretia and Iacopa the daughter of Giovanni the son of Antonio Rinaldeschi was born on the first, at the fifteenth hour]) and a dowry deposit was recorded with the Monte delle doti, which upon maturity valued 364 florins, an amount well below the post-1480 average of 739 florins; see ASF, Monte, 3747, fol. 163, where it is noted that she died in 1499, and compare A. Molho, Marriage Alliance in Late Medieval Florence (Cambridge, Mass., 1994), 157.

[37] The death was recorded in ASF, Ufficiali della Grascia, "Libro nero de' morti" (1457–1506), fol. 288[v]: "Giovanni d'Agnolo [sic] Rinaldeschi, riposto in Santa Maria maggiore. A' dì 29." Giovanni's daughters were instead on good terms with him, to judge from the provisions of his testament. He also appears to have provided financial support to one of his sons-in-law (see ASF, NA, 16790, Ser Piero di Andrea da Campi,

quarrelled with his stepmother Angela and his half-sisters over the estate. A settlement appears to have been reached after Antonio filed a suit in the court of the Podestà against his female relations, and after they countersued in the court of the Mercanzia.[38]

Although the sentence of the Eight calls him a "Florentine citizen" (*civis Florentinus*), Antonio's provincial ancestry was a factor that probably worked against him. Not only had the Rinaldeschi come to Florence from Prato relatively recently, but Antonio's grandmother was the daughter of a farrier from Empoli, where the family continued to own property. Notarial records from 1500 and 1501 show Antonio acting as procurator in the capital city for a series of persons from outlying parts of the Florentine territorial state—a mercenary from Cortona, a man and women from Barga, and a man from Montepulciano.[39] He appears to have occupied a tenuous social niche as an intermediary on behalf of provincial subjects to whom he perhaps falsely represented himself as a Florentine insider.

Antonio was clearly a dubious character. No Florentine came to his assistance or interceded on his behalf in his hour of need before the Eight

---

fol. 39ᵛ [30 December 1498], an agreement between Giovanni del Magno and Giovanni Rinaldeschi).

[38] The litigation is described in ASF, Mercanzia, 1577, unpaginated (7 September 1500). In his testament, Giovanni had charged Antonio's debts against his inheritance, reserving most of his estate to his third wife, Angela, and his daughters. Antonio renounced his father's inheritance and claimed the property as his rightful inheritance through his dead mother, Alessandra. On 11 November 1500 Antonio apparently met with one of his brothers-in-law, Giovanni del Magno, in the presence of a notary, since they were both witnesses to an unrelated notarial act, NA, 16790, fol. 231ʳ. Several days later, on 13 November 1500, an agreement was drawn up between Antonio, his sisters, and his stepmother which seems to have settled his claim (ibid., fols. 232ʳ–233ᵛ; see also ibid., fol. 272ʳ⁻ᵛ [6 April 1501]); and in April 1501 the claim on the estate of Antonio's half-sister Antonia and her relatives, through the dowry of Giovanni's second wife, Bartolommea, was also settled (ibid., fol. 272bisʳ [6 April 1501]). Antonia's settlement was possibly related to another act in which she appeared soon.

[39] On Antonio's grandmother, Antonia, see ASF, NA 16795, fol 431ʳ. For the land in Empoli see ASF, NA 19005, ins. 1, fol. 55ᵛ [1 January 1495/6]. For Antonio as procurator see ASF, NA, 19005, Ser Piero del Serra, ins. 1, fol. 86ʳ⁻ᵛ (26 April 1500); ibid., fol. 87ʳ⁻ᵛ (24 May 1500); ibid., fol. 87ʳ (2 June 1500); ibid., fol. 90ᵛ (17 November 1500). Shortly before his demise Antonio witnessed a notarial act in the *popolo* of S. Benedetto (NA, 9647, Ser Giovanni di Marco da Romena, fol. 232ʳ [3 June 1501]).

for Security. One of the documents from the Company of the Blacks called him "a great blasphemer [and] beater of his father"; the author of the *priorista* mentioned Rinaldeschi's syphilis and called him a "bestial man"; Landucci said he was a gambler; and none of the sources said anything in his favour except for the sympathetic treatment in the later panels of the Stibbert painting. So many sins were attributed to Rinaldeschi—some of them possibly imagined—that it seems reasonable to suggest he may have functioned as a kind of ritual scapegoat whose execution was a communal act of cleansing.[40] So far as is known, however, none of Rinaldeschi's misdeeds was of a type that would normally warrant the death penalty, and his virtues (aside from his apparent repentance) were hardly sufficient to attract divine intervention. The questions of the reason for his execution and of the nature of the miracle and cult associated with the image he desecrated are therefore not easy to answer.

In this connection it is worth stressing the role of the Eight for Security, which was a magistracy created in 1378, immediately after the revolt of the Ciompi, with jurisdiction over conspiracies, crimes of state, threats to public order, and crimes committed by Jews.[41] During the fifteenth century its powers grew steadily at the expense of the existing institutions for the administration of justice, especially the courts of the three itinerant foreign rectors: the Podestà, the Captain of the People, and the Executor of the Ordinances of Justice, which was abolished in 1435.[42] A Florentine law of 1478 described the authority of the Eight to proceed with full powers

> in deciding, sentencing, and terminating [cases] in whatever manner or form, as and however they freely wish, even summarily and *de facto*, even without stating generally or specifically the crime committed or the reason

----

[40] Compare, for instance, the rich tradition discussed in J. Bremmer, "Scapegoat Rituals in Ancient Greece," *Harvard Studies in Classical Philology*, 87 (1983), 299–320.

[41] On the Eight for Security, see G. Antonelli, "La magistratura degli Otto di Guardia a Firenze," *Archivio storico italiano*, 112 (1954), 3–39; A. Zorzi, *L'amministrazione della giustizia penale nella Repubblica fiorentina* (Florence, 1988), 42–45, 50–53, 67–72 and 83–89; and J. K. Brackett, *Criminal Justice and Crime in Late Renaissance Florence, 1537–1609* (Cambridge, 1992), esp. 8–21. Its members were usually elected to their two-month terms through a complicated process of scrutiny and sortition.

[42] On the competing jurisdictions of the courts of the foreign rectors see L. I. Stern, *The Criminal Law System of Medieval and Renaissance Florence* (Baltimore, 1994).

for their so doing, and without any proof, and without citing or observing any other solemnity of law, or statutes or orders or custom.[43]

As an authoritarian and centralizing magistracy, the Eight was naturally controversial, and there were many complaints against its arbitrary activities in the later fifteenth century, but under the post-1494 regime most Florentines, and also Fra Girolamo Savonarola, felt that it was more important to control the membership of the Eight than to restrict its powers.[44]

One of the most notable features of the Stibbert painting is its depiction of the authority and efficiency of the Eight in identifying and punishing Rinaldeschi. Although Rinaldeschi was arrested by the men of the Podestà, although his trial and execution took place in the Palace of the Podestà, and although the Podestà bore the expenses of the public feast on 22 July, the Podestà appears only in a policing role, while his role as investigator and judge has been taken over completely by the Eight. This is confirmed by examination of a register of the sentences of the Podestà, who was serving at the time, Messer Monaldo de' Fascioli of Orvieto, who served between 1 April and 1 October 1501.[45] Fascioli's personal coat-of-arms, crossed white swords on a field of red, appears both on the cover of this register [Figure 16], and in the Stibbert painting, where it is represented on a shield in the

---

[43] The law is published in V. Ricchioni, *La costituzione politica di Firenze ai tempi di Lorenzo il Magnifico* (Siena, 1913), 153: "procedendo . . . et poi decidendo, sententiando et terminando in quel modo et forma che et chome liberamente vorranno et etiam sommariamente et de facto etiam senza exprimere in genere o in specie al delicto o cagione che gli muovessi a così fare et senza alcuna pruova di quello et sanza citatione et sanza observare alcuna altra solemnità di legge o statuti o ordini o consuetudine introducta. . . ." Rinaldeschi's sentence (Document I) explicitly mentions this authority.

[44] Girolamo Savonarola, *Prediche sopra Ezechiele*, ed. R. Ridolfi, 2 vols. (Florence-Rome, 1955), I, 53 (8 December 1496): "Ognuno adunque facci orazione che si elegghino uomini terribili e rigidi in questo magistrato delli Otto, che, se faranno la iustizia, è liberata la città. . . ." [Let everyone pray therefore that terrifying and rigid men are elected to this magistracy of the Eight, since if they will do justice the city will be liberated . . . .]

[45] ASF, Atti del Podestà, 5547, "Liber condemnationum domini Monaldi de Fasadis de Urbe veteri," (1 April 1501–1 October 1501), unpaginated. A vernacular source from 1508, the "Libro di Ricordi scripto dal 1508 al 1540," cited by Richa, *Notizie* (n. 4 above), VIII, 251, mistook Civitavecchia (Lat.: *Civitas vetus*) for Orvieto (*Urbs vetus*). The coat-of-arms, carved in stone, is also preserved in the Bargello: see F. Fumi and C. Gado, *Stemmi nel Museo nazionale del Bargello* (Florence, 1993), 106–107, fig. 133.

arrest scene [Figure 4] and on a tiny banner in the courtyard of the Bargello [Figure 9]. Yet the register makes no mention of the Rinaldeschi case (presumably because it was handled by the Eight), and it suggests that most of the time Fascioli handled civil suits. Only once during his six-month term did he pronounce sentence in a capital case, which was the trial of a counterfeiter.

The diminished importance of the Podestà was plain to see, and less than a year after the Rinaldeschi episode, in April 1502, the offices of the Podestà and Captain of the People were abolished and replaced by the Council of Justice, later known as the Ruota, with competence in civil affairs. Criminal jurisdiction thus passed entirely to the Eight for Security.[46] It is not therefore surprising that they took the initiative in the case of Rinaldeschi, though their reasons for doing so require further explanation.

---

[46] By a law of 15 April 1502, Zorzi, *L'amministrazione* (n. 41 above), 103; discussed also in Antonelli, "La magistratura" (n. 41 above), 29, and L. Martines, *Lawyers and Statecraft in Renaissance Florence* (Princeton, 1968), 137–142.

CHAPTER 2
THE NATURE OF THE OFFENCE

Rinaldeschi's story deserves the attention of historians for several reasons besides its human interest and pathos. Above all, it is an exceptionally well documented instance of the interaction of legal institutions,[1] political circumstances, and popular religious feelings, and it needs to be understood in the light of Florentine history in the years immediately following the death of Savonarola in 1498. The record of Rinaldeschi's trial by the Eight for Security said that his offences were

> against the form of canon law, of the statutes and ordinances of the Commune of Florence, and good behaviour (*bonos mores*). Wishing therefore to punish the said Antonius for such a serious crime (*excessus*), according to his offences (*demerita*), since no one should be lord of his limbs and of his own life, and in order that his punishment might be an example for others and that the name of the blessed, glorious Virgin may be held in honour,

they condemned him to death. It is hard to judge from this whether his primary offence was gambling ("against ... the statutes ... of Florence"), attempted suicide ("since no one should be lord of his limbs and of his own life") or blasphemy ("that the name of the blessed, glorious Virgin may be held in honour").[2] We must take a closer look at each of these charges, which were doubtless associated in the minds of the judges.

Of his three offences—gambling, attempted suicide and blasphemy—, the least serious was gambling, though it was the root cause of Rinaldeschi's problems.[3] Gambling was ubiquitous in medieval soci-

---

[1] T. Kuehn, *Law, Family and Women: Toward a Legal Anthropology of Renaissance Italy* (Chicago, 1991), 7, argues for the need "to bring law to bear in the reading of the generally legal sources for Florentine social history."

[2] In the Appendix, Document I.

[3] See the three articles originally published in 1886–1893 and reprinted in L. Zdekauer, *Il gioco d'azzardo nel medioevo italiano* (Florence, 1993), of which the introduction, by G. Ortalli, is entitled "Between interdiction and tolerance"; R. Orioli, "Bestemmie e gioco d'azzardo nel medioevo," *Abstracta*, 1: 4 (1986), 48–53; W. Tauber, *Das Würfelspiel im Mittelalter und in der frühen Neuzeit. Eine kultur-und sprachgeschichtliche Darstellung* (Frankfurt a.M., 1987), esp. 46–67, on the warnings and

ety, and in spite of many prohibitions and restrictions, it was generally tolerated and almost never punished by death. The decree of the Fourth Lateran Council in 1215 forbidding clerics to gamble or to participate in games of chance said nothing about gambling by laymen,[4] and some late fourteenth-century inquisitorial records from Bologna show that the church took gambling much less seriously than the blasphemy which often accompanied it.[5] Gamblers at the moment of play often called on God and, when they lost, blamed the Virgin, who thus took on the character of Dame Fortune and Lady Luck.

Bartholomew of Trent in his *Book of Miracles of the Blessed Virgin Mary*, which dates from the second quarter of the thirteenth century, included a story about a gambler in Trent who, after losing at play, attacked an image of the crucifixion with a knife, inflicting "more wounds than the crucifiers," and who, eight days later, killed himself with the same knife at Bolzano.[6] In Florence, before 1320, a disappointed gambler threw a dagger at an image of the Virgin, causing it to bleed, and was hanged in the Piazza of S. Maria Novella.[7] In 1413 a

---

prohibitions against gambling and dicing; J.-M. Mehl, *Les jeux au royaume de France du XIIIe au début du XVIe siècle* (Paris, 1990), 76–98 on dicing; A. Rizzi, *Ludus/ludere. Giocare in Italia alla fine del medio evo*, Ludica: collana di storia del gioco 3 (Treviso-Rome, 1995); and G. Mentgen, "Alltagsgeschichte und Geschichte der Juden. Die Juden und das Glücksspiel im Mittelalter," *Historische Zeitschrift*, 274 (2002), 25–60. For communal statutes on gambling, see *Statuta civitatis Aquaram* (Acqui, 1618), 62; *Gli statuti di Genola*, ed. R. Comba (Turin, 1970), 82–83; and *Statuta Ferrrariae, anno MCCLXXVII*, ed. W. Montorsi (Ferrara, 1955), 349–355. (We owe these references to James Powell.) For Florence, see J. Kohler and G. degli Azzi, *Das Florentiner Strafrecht des XIV. Jahrhunderts* (Mannheim-Leipzig, 1909), 10–13 (1322–1325), 86 (1379), and 207; and U. Dorini, *Il diritto penale e la delinquenza in Firenze nel sec. XIV* (Lucca, n.d. [but 1923]), 247–248.

[4] IV Lateran 1215, c. 16, in *Conciliorum oecumenicorum decreta*, ed. Giuseppe Alberigo et al., 3rd ed. (Bologna, 1973), 243.

[5] Orioli, "Bestemmie" (n. 3 above), 52–53. On the association of gambling with blasphemy, see *Corpus iuris civilis*, II: *Codex Iustinianus*, III, 43.1, ed. P. Krueger (Berlin, 1954), 147; *Index tractatum universi iuris*, I (Venice, 1585), 129^v; and, for the early modern period O. Christin, "Matériaux pour servir à l'histoire du blasphème [II]," *Bulletin d'information de la Mission historique française en Allemagne*, 32 (1996), 67, 70, and 73.

[6] A. Dondaine, "Barthélemy de Trente, O.P.," *Archivum Fratrum Praedicatorum*, 45 (1975), 79–105 (98).

[7] J. W. Brown, *The Dominican Church of Santa Maria Novella at Florence* (Edinburgh, 1902), 81, with references in n. 2 to the manuscript of Vincenzo Fineschi's memorials of Santa Maria Novella from 1221 to 1320; and W. Hood, *Fra Angelico at San Marco*

gambler near Pisa who twice attacked images of the Virgin with a knife—telling her "I can't do anything worse to you; if I were able to, I would do it!"—was sentenced to be burned to death in a wooden cage, but this punishment (commuted to decapitation) was directed in part at his other crimes, since he was also convicted of two counts of incest.[8]

The most interesting parallels to the story of Rinaldeschi are found in the *Cantigas de Santa Maria* of Alfonso the Wise, which were written between 1257 and 1283 and of which two of the four known manuscripts are illustrated.[9] Song 136 recounts, in the words of the preamble,

> how in the land of Apulia, in a city called Foggia, a woman was playing at dice with some companions in front of a church. Because she lost, she threw a stone at the Holy Child held by the statue of Holy Mary, who raised her arm and received the blow.

According to the text of the song, the statue was of marble and greatly revered, the event took place during the reign of Conrad IV (1250–1254), and the woman, a German, was playing dice with some of his soldiers. When she threw a stone at the Child, the Virgin raised her arm and "The stone chipped a little hole in her elbow, which could be seen there forever after as an example." When it was repaired, "The arm was in no way altered or put back as it was before, for God wished it to remain as a sign."[10] The illustration in the Escorial Codex (Figure 17) is divided into six scenes beginning, at the top left, with the statue

---

(New Haven, 1993), 158 and 314 n. 23.

[8] The original sentence was published by G. Brucker, *Firenze nel Rinascimento* (Florence, 1980), 325–329, and in translation in *The Society of Renaissance Florence: A Documentary Study*, ed. G. Brucker (New York, 1971), 150–153.

[9] *Cantigas de Santa María. Edición facsímil del Códice T. I. 1 de la Biblioteca de San Lorenzo el Real de El Escorial. Siglo XIII* (Madrid, 1979) (the Escorial Codex) and *Cantigas de Santa Maria. Edición facsímil del Códice B. R. 20 de la Biblioteca Nazionale Centrale de Florencia. Siglo XIII*, 2 vols. (Madrid, 1989) (the Florence Codex). See David Flory, *Marian Representations in the Miracle Tales of Thirteenth-Century Spain and France* (Washington, D.C., 2000), 110–129. The *Cantigas* are cited here from *Songs of Holy Mary of Alfonso X, the Wise*, trans. K. Kulp-Hill (Tempe, Ariz., 2000). On gambling in Spain, where it was profitable to the king and controlled by law but not prohibited (or even disapproved of), see D. E. Carpenter, "Fickle Fortune: Gambling in Medieval Spain," *Studies in Philology*, 85 (1988), 267–278, and idem, " 'Alea jacta est': At the Gaming Table with Alfonso the Learned," *Journal of Medieval History*, 24 (1998), 333–345.

[10] *Songs* (n. 9 above), 169.

of the Virgin and Child set into a niche in the wall of the church, in front of which there is a group of gamblers, including a woman, behind whom a devil lurks. The second scene shows her throwing the stone; the third, the Virgin with her arm raised to protect the Child and struck by the stone; the fourth, the woman being taken before the king; the fifth, her being dragged by a horse, presumably until she was dead; and the sixth, the restoration of the statue.

A similar story is told in Song 294, where "A woman who was playing dice in Apulia threw a stone at the statue of the Holy Mary because she had lost, and an angel of stone which was there reached out its hand and received the blow." The woman was seized and thrown into a fire. "The angel ever after held its hand outstretched ... For this reason that statue was thereafter held in much greater esteem by all those people than it ever was before." The illustration in the Florence Codex (Figure 18), also in six scenes, shows, first, the façade of the church with the statue of the Virgin and Child flanked by two angels above the door and then, successively, the gamblers, the woman throwing the stone, the remonstrances of the onlookers, her arrest, and her funeral pyre. There is no devil, as in the Escorial illustration to *Cantiga* 136, and no visible change in the position of the angel's hand. Another song in the *Cantigas* related "How a gambler [in Catalonia] shot an arrow with his crossbow at the sky in anger because he had lost. He thought he would wound God or Holy Mary", but after the arrow came down covered with blood he entered a religious order (Figure 19).[11]

In spite of the resemblances between these stories and that of Rinaldeschi, they were independent and show the association of gambling with blasphemy and sacrilege.[12] They are concerned less with

---

[11] Ibid., 354 and 188 (no. 154). In no. 238 (ibid., 287–288) a minstrel in Portugal played at dice and cursed God and the Virgin, spitting when a priest came by with the Corpus Christi. He was squeezed by the devil until he was completely twisted. On gamblers in Marian miracles, see E. G. Grigione, "L'empio giocatore nelle leggende dell'*Atlante mariano*," *Il santo*, 23 (1983), 345–341, and Carpenter, " 'Alea' " (n. 9 above), 335.

[12] Other stories in which gambling is associated with blasphemy are found in *The Exempla of Jacques de Vitry*, ed. T. F. Crane, Publications of the Folk-lore Society 26 (London, 1890), 91, no. 218, and John Major, *Magnum speculum exemplorum* (Douai, 1624), 90–92, nos. 4 and 7, and 602, no. 9. See F. C. Tubach, *Index exemplorum*, Folklore Fellows Communications 204 (Helsinki, 1969), 158, 179, and 219, nos. 1949, 2240, and 2789. On the association of gambling with suicide: see C. Moore, *A Full Inquiry into the Subject of Suicide*, 2 vols. (London, 1790), I, 24–25, and II, 286–292,

gambling itself, which they take for granted, than with its consequences. While the attitude in Italy may have changed in the fifteenth century owing to the influence of St. Antoninus, archbishop of Florence, and St. Bernardino of Siena, when there was a rash of decrees against gambling and arrests for gambling in Florence,[13] there is no evidence that the death penalty was ever imposed, that Rinaldeschi's gambling counted heavily against him, or that he was executed on this account.

The attempted suicide was a more serious matter.[14] The right of individuals to take their own lives was recognized in antiquity and in Roman law. Only under special circumstances, such as to avoid merited disgrace, were soldiers forbidden under pain of death to injure or try to kill themselves.[15] In Christian teaching, on the other hand, suicide was considered a mortal sin, and its success or failure in principle had no bearing on its moral content. Attempted suicide was rarely discussed, however, and was not severely punished. The fourth canon of the Sixteenth Council of Toledo in 693 prescribed a punishment of excommunication for two months, and according to the Penitential of Vigila

---

which is mostly concerned with the early modern period.

[13] Zdekauer, *Gioco d'azzardo* (n. 3 above), 71; A. Zorzi, "Battagliole e giochi d'azzardo a Firenze nel tardo Medioevo: due pratiche sociali tra disciplinamento e repressione," in *Gioco e giustizia nell'Italia di comune*, ed. G. Ortalli, Ludica: collana di storia del gioco 1 (Treviso-Rome, 1993), 86–90; and Rizzi, *Ludus* (n. 3 above), 87 and 110–113. A Florentine law of 17 April 1454 (copy in ASF, OGB, 224, fols. 8ᵛ–9ᵛ) gave the Eight full authority over gambling, even in private houses; however, according to Brackett, *Criminal Justice* (above, ch.1 n. 41), 117, the records of the Eight suggest "that the authorities did not expect to eradicate, but only to control, this addiction."

[14] On suicide in the Middle Ages, see F. Bourquelot, "Recherches sur les opinions et la législation en matière de mort volontaire pendant le moyen âge," *Bibliothèque de l'École des chartes*, 3 (1841–1842), 539–560, and 4 (1842–1843), 242–266 and 456–475, and A. Murray, *Suicide in the Middle Ages*, II: *The Curse on Self-Murder* (Oxford, 2000), of which we saw a preliminary version of the chapter on attempted suicide before the publication of our 1998 article. J.-C. Schmitt, "Le suicide au moyen âge," *Annales, E.S.C.*, 31 (1976), 3–28, and G. Minois, *History of Suicide: Voluntary Death in Western Culture*, tr. L. Cochrane (Baltimore, 1999) do not discuss attempted suicide.

[15] Justinian, *Digest*, XLVIII, 19.38.12 and XLIX, 16.6.7, ed. T. Mommsen (Berlin, 1870; repr. 1963), 854 and 895. On these laws see Bourquelot, "Recherches" (n. 14 above), 545–546; A. Berger, *Encyclopedic Dictionary of Roman Law*, Transactions of the American Philosophical Society, n.s., 43:2 (Philadelphia, 1953), 723; and A. J. Droge and J. D. Tabor, *A Noble Death: Suicide and Martyrdom among Christians and Jews in Antiquity* (San Francisco, 1992), esp. 167–183 on "The Augustinian Reversal" of the previously positive view of suicide.

of Avila, which was written in Spain in the early ninth century, "He who wishes to kill himself by hanging or in some other way and whom God does not abandon to be killed shall for this thing do penance for five years."[16]

In practice attempted suicide was treated with sympathy rather than severity. Martin of Tours revived by prayer and bodily contact a young slave (*seruulus*) who tried to kill himself with a noose and who apparently suffered no subsequent punishment.[17] There are many references in medieval literature to heroes who at one time or another contemplated suicide, and also, especially in moral tales or *exempla*, to people who tried to kill themselves.[18] Guibert of Nogent in his account of his own life included a story of a monk who was inspired by the Devil to cut his own throat and was brought to life through the intervention of St. James, who was "mindful of his intention". He later said that while he was dead he had been brought before God and been pardoned by the Virgin.[19] This and similar stories reflect the importance attributed to intention in the moral theology of the twelfth and thirteenth centuries. Theologians were not always so forgiving. Abelard, who laid great stress on intention in assigning moral responsibility, said in a letter to Heloise that Origen by mutilating himself was guilty of homicide.[20]

---

[16] XVI Toledo 693, c. 4, in *Sacrorum conciliorum nova et amplissima collectio*, ed. G. D. Mansi, 31 vols. (Florence-Venice, 1759–1798), XII, 71–72, and *Poenitentiale Vigilanuum*, in *Die Bussordnungen der abendländischen Kirche*, ed. F. W. H. Wasserschleben (Halle, 1851), 530, tr. J. T. McNeill and H. M. Gamer, *Medieval Handbooks of Penance*, Records of Civilization 29 (New York, 1938), 291. See Bourquelot, "Recherches" (n. 14 above), 555, who said there were no prescriptions against attempted suicide in the canons of the early councils, and Murray, *Suicide* (n. 14 above), II, 400–401, who also draws attention to the indirect evidence of the Old Norse Eidsivathinglaw, which denied Christian burial to a suicide "if he dies of it", but not apparently if he lived.

[17] Sulpicius Severus, *Vita S. Martini*, 8:1, ed. J. Fontaine, 3 vols., Sources chrétiennes 133–135 (Paris, 1967–1969), I, 270.

[18] M.-N. Lefay-Toury, *La tentation du suicide dans le roman français du XIIe siècle* (Paris, 1979).

[19] Guibert of Nogent, *De vita sua*, III, 19, ed. G. Bourgin, Collection de textes pour servir à l'étude et à l'enseignement de l'histoire 40 (Paris, 1907), 221. Other accounts of the compassionate treatment of attempted suicides are found in *Libellus Monasteriensis de miraculis s. Luidgeri*, 16, in *Westfälisches Urkunden-Buch: Addimenta*, ed. R. Wilmans (Münster, 1877), 110, and Caesarius of Heisterbach, *Dialogus miraculorum*, IV, 40 and 45, ed. J. Strange, 2 vols. (Cologne-Bonn-Brussels, 1851), I, 209 and 212–213. See Bourquelot, "Recherches" (n. 14 above), 252.

[20] Abelard, *Ep.* 4 to Heloise, ed. J. T. Muckle, "The Personal Letters between

There was at the same time a growing interest among jurists in the criminality of attempted suicide, which was included with crimes like high treason, raping a nun, and various types of homicide. Roger in his *Summa codicis*, which dates from about 1160, held that someone who tried to kill himself should be punished "because he who does not spare himself much less spares another,"[21] and Peter of Belleperche, chancellor to King Philip IV of France, wrote in his commentary on the Code that

> If someone wished to kill himself [and] he was opposed and prevented from killing himself, I say that he should be hanged, because the law says that someone who wishes to kill another, though he cannot, should be punished as for homicide, therefore [likewise] if he wishes to kill himself.

And he cited the *lex Cornelia* on murderers, which held that "The intention is taken for the deed."[22]

There is something illogical, however, in killing people who have tried unsuccessfully to kill themselves, and some jurists were less severe than Peter of Belleperche. Jean Bouthillier, in his influential *Somme rurale*, which was written about 1370, said that someone who attempted to kill himself or another person deserved to be severely punished but not put to death, provided he confessed and repented, but he concluded that "If it was through an unaccomplished work of despair, and of which the man repented, know that the person should be sent to confession and contrition according to spiritual counsel and to spiritual penance"; and Jean Feu of Orléans (1477–1547) held those who attempted to kill themselves out of weariness with life, grief, anger, illness, shame, drunkenness, or wantonness should not be punished.[23]

Abelard and Heloise," *Mediaeval Studies*, 15 (1953), 90.

[21] Roger, *Summa codicis*, IX, 42, in *Scripta anecdota glossatorum*, ed. G.B. Palmieri, Bibliotheca iuridica Medii Aevi 1 (Bologna, 1914), 227.

[22] Peter of Belleperche (Bellapertica), *Super IX libros codicis*, on *Code*, VI, 22 (Paris, 1569; repr. 1968), fol. 274ᵛ, cf. his commentary on *Code*, IX, 16 (the *lex Cornelia* on murderers) and IX, 50 (the property of suicides), ibid., fols. 402ʳ and 407ʳ. For the *lex Cornelia*, see *Code*, IX, 16, in *Codex Iustinianus* (n. 5 above), 379, and *Digest*, XXXXVIII, 8, 7, ed. Mommsen (n. 15 above), 820, which was cited by Roger, *Summa codicis*, IX, 13, ed. Palmieri (n. 21 above), 217. These sources are cited by Murray, *Suicide* (n. 14 above) in his chapter on attempted suicide.

[23] Jean Boutillier, *Somme rurale*, 39 (Paris, 1611), 273, and Jean Feu (Joannes Igneus), *Commentarii in titulum de Sillaniano et Claudiano senatus consulto* (Lyon-Orléans, 1539), fol. 93v. On attempted suicide, see Bourquelot, "Recherches" (n. 14 above), 262; and, generally, C. Calisse, *A History of Italian Law*, tr. L. Register (London, 1928), 412.

The records of actual cases of attempted suicide show that the culprits were usually let off with an admonition or fine or were condemned to a variety of punishments, all far short of execution.[24] There were two cases of attempted suicide in fourteenth-century Florence, one in 1300 and another in 1379, when a poor man stabbed himself in the neck "with the spirit and intention of killing himself" and was fined two hundred lire and imprisoned, apparently for a short time, when he was unable to pay.[25] Rinaldeschi's judges may have known the view of Savonarola that the challengers in the planned ordeal by fire in 1498 were "homicides of themselves (*homicidi di se medesimi*), since they were sure to die."[26] It is also possible that they included the charge of attempted suicide because it had been seen by many competent witnesses and offered a secure legal basis for Rinaldeschi's conviction, since attempted suicide was considered an implicit confession.[27] There is no serious reason to believe, however, that Rinaldeschi was put to death because he tried to kill himself, although it undoubtedly counted against him.

Among the charges brought against Joan of Arc was the threat to kill herself; P. Champion, *Procès de condemnation de Jeanne d'Arc*, 2 vols. (Paris, 1920–1921), II, 163–164 and 263, cf. 200–201.

[24] Murray, *Suicide* (n. 14 above), II, 418 and 412, remarked on "the apparent indifference to attempted suicide." He found no attempted suicide who was put to death, though they might be punished in the secular courts. Francesco Guicciardini made no reference to attempted suicide in his treatise *Del suicidio per ragione di libertà o di servitù*, in *Opere inedite di Francesco Guicciardini*, ed. P. and L. Guicciardini (Florence, 1867), 382–388. Cf. O. Bernstein, *Die Bestrafung des Selbstmords und ihr Ende*, Strafrechtliche Abhandlung 78 (Breslau, 1907), 8 and 15, on later punishments for attempted suicide in Prussia and Bohemia.

[25] Kohler and degli Azzi, *Florentiner Strafrecht* (n. 3 above), 88–89, cf. 203. See Murray, *Suicide* (n. 14 above), II, 419–420; R. Davidsohn, *Geschichte von Florenz*, 4 vols. (Berlin, 1896–1927), IV: 1, 312, and (generally on suicide in Florence), IV: 3, 381–382; and Dorini, *Diritto penale* (n. 3 above), 135. Moore, *Suicide* (n. 12 above), II, 167–169, cited an example of a case in England of attempted suicide owing to poverty.

[26] Johannes Burckard, *Liber notarum*, ed. E. Celani, 2 vols., Rerum italicarum scriptores, 2nd ed., XXXII:1 (Città di Castello, 1907–1942), II, 84. See Bourquelot, "Recherches" (n. 14 above), 463. We are indebted to Donald Weinstein for help on this point.

[27] Had Rinaldeschi not confessed, he would presumably have been tortured, since in the Roman tradition two eyewitnesses were needed for conviction of a capital crime: see E. Peters, *Inquisition* (Berkeley-Los Angeles, 1988), 64–65, and Murray, *Suicide* (n. 14 above), II, 171.

Rinaldeschi's most egregious offence, and the probable cause of his execution, was blasphemy and sacrilege.[28] The record of his trial said that after losing his money, he "blasphemed himself and the name of the glorious virgin mother Mary and used words that are better kept silent," and that "with the spirit and intention of committing and perpetrating another unspeakable and horrible offence" he threw dung at the image of the Virgin "to its very great dishonour and disgrace and to the shame of the Christian faith." He was condemned, the record continued later, in order "that the name of the blessed, glorious Virgin may be held in honour," and, according to one record of the Company of the Blacks, "because in despair he befouled with dung the figure of Our Lady at the Alberighi" (Appendix, Document III). These references to dishonouring the Virgin emphasize the heinousness of Rinaldeschi's crime. Its local impact may be judged by a comparison with the ritual of house-scorning, in which mud, ink, blood, or excrement were thrown at the house of an enemy, who had to clean it off as soon as possible in order to vindicate his honour.[29]

The term blasphemy, though often used to apply only to speech, in fact covers a wide variety of verbal and physical abuse and was severely condemned in the Old Testament and in ancient civil law, where blasphemy and sacrilege were closely linked to treason or *laesa maiestas*, which was later equated with *laesa religio*.[30] Medieval theologians and

---

[28] D. Lawton, *Blasphemy* (Philadelphia, 1993), 16, writes that "the word is not stably differential from heresy, apostasy and sacrilege" and that " 'Blasphemy' comprises swearing, gambling, drinking, impiety, slander, sexual deviance, heresy, preaching against the Gospel, sacrilege, and any hypocrisy, defamation or rebellion against God." See (on the pre-Christian period) R. Parker, *Miasma: Pollution and Purification in Early Greek Religion* (Oxford, 1983), 144–190; A. Molien in the *Dictionnaire de droit canonique*, II, col. 902, citing Origen and Augustine; C. Casagrande and S. Vecchio, *I peccati della lingua. Disciplina ed etica della parola nella cultura medievale* (Rome, 1987), 229–240, who concentrate on verbal blasphemy but acknowledge that in common usage blasphemy included "colpe di diversa natura" (229); and, on France, O. Christin, "Sur la condamnation du blasphème (XVIe–XVIIe siècles)," *Revue d'histoire de l'église de France*, 80 (1994), 43–64 (45, on "la polysémie du terme de blasphème" in the late medieval and early modern periods), and C. Leveleux, *La parole interdite. Le blasphème dans la France médiévale (XIIIe–XVIe siècles): du péché au crime* (Paris, 2001).

[29] See E. Cohen, "Honor and Gender in the Streets of Early Modern Rome," *Journal of Interdisciplinary History*, 22 (1992), 597–625 (603); cf. 606 and 616 for other references to throwing excrement and 623 on the haste in cleaning.

[30] F. Lear, "Blasphemy in the *Lex Romana Curiensis*" (1931), repr. in his *Treason in Roman and Germanic Law* (Austin, 1965), 175, said that there was "a broad highway

jurists took seriously the command in Leviticus 24.16 that "He that blasphemeth the name of the Lord, dying let him die." Gregory the Great in the *Dialogues* told the story of a small boy who, unrestrained by his father, "was accustomed to blaspheme the majesty of God whenever anything was contrary to his wishes" and who, dying with blasphemy on his lips, went to hell.[31] Peter Comestor defined blasphemy (in contrast to contumely and iniquity) as sin against God Himself and the religion of the faith, and for Thomas Aquinas blasphemy was by its nature a mortal sin and the most serious of all sins.[32] The assumption that blasphemers would be punished by divine rather than human agency may account for the lack of any generally accepted, specific distinctions between blasphemy and sacrilege in either canon or civil law.

The first general civil law against blasphemy was in the *Novella* of Justinian, who decreed that blasphemers should be punished first by making themselves unworthy of God's mercy and then by tortures. According to the so-called epitome of Julian compiled in the mid-sixth century, anyone who blasphemed against God would be subject to execution.[33] In the late medieval and early modern period, jurists generally held that the punishment for blasphemy was death. Bertachinus, in his *Repertorium*, published in 1539, concluded that "In the common law (*de iure communi*) the blasphemer is punished by capital punishment";[34] and Domenico Toschi (d. 1620) devoted a special

---

running from sedition and treason against land and folk through high treason and related crimes of majesty ... to sacrilege, impiety, blasphemy, and heresy." See 179–180 on blasphemy in the Vulgate.

31 Gregory the Great, *Dialogi*, IV, 19, ed. A. de Vogüé, 3 vols., Sources chrétiennes 251, 260, 265 (Paris, 1978–1980), III, 72–74.

32 Peter Comestor, *Sermo in festo S. Magdalenae*, among the works of Hildebert of Lavardin, in *Patrologia Latina*, CLXXI, col. 675B, and Thomas Aquinas, *Summa theologiae*, 2.2, Qu. 13, art. 2 and 3 (Marietti ed., 6 vols. [Turin, 1938], III, 79).

33 Justinian, *Novella*, LXXVII, 1.1, in *Corpus iuris civilis*, III: *Novellae*, ed. R. Schoell (Berlin, 1954), 382, and *Iuliani epitome latina Novellarum Iustiniani*, Const. LXXI, ed. G. Haenel (Osnabrück, 1873, repr. 1965), 95, who went on to decree the same punishment for someone who did not denounce a blasphemer. See also *Dict. de droit can.* (n. 28 above), II, col. 912.

34 Giovanni Bertacchini of Fermo, *Repertorium*, I (Lyon, 1539), fol. 166ʳ, who cited, in addition to Bartolus and Baldus, the jurisconsults Jacopo Bottrigari of Bologna (d. 1347), Angelo Giambiglioni of Arezzo (d. 1461), and Alessandro Tartagni of Imola (d. 1477). See also *Index tractatum* (n. 5 above), fol. 129ᵛ: "Blasphemans, consuetudine, potest ad mortem damnari, quando blasphemia est publica." [A blaspheming person, by custom, can be condemned to death, if the blasphemy is public.]

section of his book on the practical conclusions of law to the question of whether blasphemy was an ecclesiastical or secular crime and decided, citing Giulio Claro (d. 1575), that it was a mixed crime that could be punished in either court, but not in both. According to both divine and civil law, he wrote, death is the penalty for blasphemy, and "The blasphemer is punished by capital punishment and the ultimate suffering."[35]

These works show the influence of the Old Testament and Roman law, but their writers did not live entirely in the realm of theological and legal theory. They recognized that not all blasphemers could be executed and therefore drew many distinctions in their definitions of blasphemy. Scholastic theologians divided blasphemy into attributive, derogative, and usurpative. Alessandro Tartagni (d. 1477) distinguished simple from habitual blasphemy, which had to be repeated more than three times and proved by several witnesses.[36] Toschi, again citing Giulio Claro, wrote that the punishment of death was "not customarily observed ... because if all blasphemers were punished with the penalty of death, few people would remain."[37] Some lawyers argued that blasphemy resulting from anger or drunkenness should not be punished at all. In the seventeenth century the Florentine lawyer Marco Antonio Savelli of Modigliana, whose *Summa diversarum tractatuum* was based on earlier sources, said that although the penalties for blasphemy included death "just as the punishment of death is imposed by the law of Caesar," there were many different opinions and exceptions based on the type of blasphemy and the status of the blasphemer.[38]

Very little is known about civil prosecution for blasphemy in the Italian city-states. No cases of blasphemy were brought before the Podestà in Bologna between 1385 and 1400. In the fifteenth century blasphemy, like gambling, was increasingly punished by pecuniary rather than corporal penalties – "a sort of taxation," as Zorzi called it, on deviant

---

We are indebted to Domenico Maffei and Peter Weimar for help in identifying these and other authors.

[35] Domenico Toschi, *Practicae conclusiones iuris*, 4th ed., I (Lyon, 1661), 319. See generally Calisse, *History* (n. 23 above), 412.

[36] Alessandro Tartagni, *Consiliorum seu responsorum libri*, I, cons. 72, and VI, cons. 233, adn. (Frankfurt, 1610), I, 154, and II, 315.

[37] Toschi, *Practicae* (n. 35 above), 319.

[38] Marco Antonio Savelli of Modigliana, *Summa diversorum tractatuum*, I (Parma, 1717), 172–173, citing Pietro Caballo, *Resolutiones criminales*, cas. 296, no. 32 (Venice, 1644), 260a. Caballo was a judge in Florence who died in 1616.

but widely tolerated types of behaviour.[39] In Florence a civil statute in 1415 established that "Anyone who blasphemes the name of our Lord Jesus Christ or any saint, male or female, will be fined one hundred lire common coinage and if he cannot pay the fine made for it he should be whipped naked in broad daylight (*de die*) and be beaten through the city of Florence."[40] In 1542 the fines were established at two hundred lire for the first offence, three hundred for the second, and five hundred for the third, to which might be added, progressively, piercing the tongue and exile for between six and twelve months, and a parade on a donkey and two years in the galleys.[41] North of the Alps in the sixteenth and seventeenth centuries blasphemy was punished by a gradation from pecuniary to corporal penalties, but at the same time the laws took into consideration extenuating circumstances, such as alcohol and anger.[42]

Severe punishments were not unknown, however, and often depended on individual circumstances, as in the case of the gambler decapitated in Pisa in 1413 (mentioned on pp. 36–37 above). A fifteenth-century statute of Badia Tedalda, a feudal holding under the protection of Florence, punished blasphemers against God and the

---

[39] Zorzi, "Le esecuzioni" (above, ch. 1 n. 3), 14.

[40] *Statuta populi et communis Florentiae*, 3 vols. (Freiburg [but Florence], 1771–1781), I, 256–257 (III, rub. 38). Note that the same 1415 statute (I, 371 [III, rub. 166]) classified the throwing of stones at Florence's most important churches and their holy images as a lesser crime, to be punished with a fine of 25 lire and the repair of any damage. See also, Brackett, *Criminal Justice* (above, ch. 1 n. 41), 129; and, for earlier Florentine statutes on blasphemy, Dorini, *Diritto penale* (n. 3 above), 129–130. For other communal statutes on blasphemy, see *Gli statuti del commune di Treviso, sec. XIII–XIV*, ed. B. Detto (Rome, 1984), 571–572, and *Statuta ... Aquarum* (n. 3 above), 62. On the strengthening of blasphemy statutes and their enforcement in Venice and throughout Europe in the early sixteenth century, see R. Derosas, "Moralità e giustizia a Venezia del '500–'600. Gli esecutori contro la bestemmia," in *Stato, società e giustizia nella Repubblica veneta (sec. XV–XVIII)*, 2 vols., ed. G. Cozzi (Milan, 1980–1985), I, 431–528.

[41] Brackett, *Criminal Justice* (above, ch. 1 n. 41), 129. According to N. Terpstra, "Confraternities and Public Charity: Modes of Civic Welfare in Early Modern Italy," in J. P. Donnelly, S.J. and M. W. Maher, S. J., eds., *Confraternities and Catholic Reform in Italy, France, and Spain*, Sixteenth Century Essays and Studies 44 (Kirksville, 1999), 113–114, beginning in 1542 one third of the fines for blasphemy in Florence were directed toward poor relief.

[42] For legislation on blasphemy in the sixteenth and seventeenth centuries, see Christin, "Sur la condemnation" (n. 28 above), 49, and, generally, his articles on "Matériaux [I–II]" (n. 5 above), 29 (1994), 56–67, and 32 (1996), 67–85.

Virgin with a fine of 10 lire common coinage, while blasphemers against "God's saints" received a lesser fine equivalent to 5 lire.[43] A blasphemer at Florence in 1512 was sentenced to three years banishment after being led through the streets of the city with a spike through his tongue.[44] According to a letter of 1543, Duke Cosimo I de' Medici sometimes excused blasphemers from corporal punishment and required them to pay only the stipulated fine, provided that they had not blasphemed a particular saint, and duchess Eleonora interceded with her husband on behalf of one Piero del Quadro, who had been condemned to a fine of two hundred lire and piercing of his tongue for saying "Christ's cunt!" (*potta di Cristo*), but who was "old, poor, and burdened with a family."[45] His punishment was reduced because no saint had been offended, but only Christ, who was presumably all-forgiving.

Ecclesiastical law tended to be more lenient, or perhaps more realistic, than civil law with regard to blasphemy. According to the Second Council of Ravenna in 1311, first offenders should be excluded from the church for a month and repeaters should be denied Christian burial.[46] The Bolognese inquisitorial records cited above show that the

---

[43] *Gli statuti quattrocenteschi di Badia Tedalda e di Pratieghi*, eds. M. Laurenti and P. Mariani Biagini (Florence, 1992), 61, where 100 soldi = five lire.

[44] ASF, OGB, 230, fol. 23^r (8 April 1511).

[45] Letter from Bastiano Bindi to Lorenzo Pagni, ASF, Mediceo del Principato, 1176b, fol. 658^r (6 June 1543): "Per una di vostra S.^{tia} di Pietrasanta de' iiii del presente ho visto quanto quella mi comanda, per parte della Ex.^{tia} della duchessa, circa a Piero del Quadro, condemnato in lire 200 et perforatione della lingua per havere detto 'potta di Christo', come si contiene nella sua querela et confessione: di che la ex.tia del ducha, quando e' non fussi bestemmia d'alcuno santo, qualche volta ha levato la pena corporale et fatto pagare la pecuniaria [...]. Et di questo caso proprio se n'è scripto a sua ex.^{tia} et narrato a pieno la qualità della bestemmia, et come Piero è vechio, povero, et charicho di famiglia. Et tuttavia si aspecta quella ne aviserà sua ex.^{tia} Illma." [In a letter of your Lordship's from Pietrasanta of the 4th of this month I have seen what your lordship commands of me on behalf of her Excellency the Duchess concerning Piero del Quadro, who was condemned with a 200 lire fine and perforation of the tongue for having said "Christ's cunt!" as is contained in his appeal and his confession: for which the Excellency of the Duke, if there was no blasphemy of any saint, has sometimes lifted the corporal penalty and insisted on the pecuniary one... And as to this particular case, his Excellency was informed of it, and told fully the nature of the blasphemy, and how Piero is old, poor and burdened with a family. And all the same we await what his most Illustrious Excellency will advise concerning it.]

[46] II Ravenna 1311, c. 27, in Mansi, *Collectio* (n. 16 above), XXV, cols. 471–472. The council of Paris in 1429, cc. 22 and 26, punished the first offence with a week in prison on bread and water the second with two weeks, and the third with the

punishments imposed for blasphemy included fasting, reciting the Our
Father, attending masses in particular churches, and, for more serious
cases, penitential pilgrimages. Blasphemy of this sort was often associated
with gambling.[47] In 1514 the Fifth Lateran Council established various
scales of punishments, depending on the number of offences and in
addition to any penances imposed *in foro conscientiae*, for blasphemers who
held public offices, for clerics and priests, for noblemen, and for non-no-
blemen and plebeians, who were punished for more than two offences
by spending a day in front of the principal church wearing the hat of
infamy (*mitra infamiae*), probably a sort of dunce's cap. Hardened blasphemers might be sent to prison or to the galleys. Judges and rulers who
enforced these punishments, and informers, were rewarded with a third
of the fines and with an indulgence of ten years.[48]

   Three years later the provincial synod held in Florence repeated
the decree of the Fifth Lateran Council and added two chapters, one
saying that divine majesty was as much injured by what was done to
images as "to him whom the image represents" and another decreeing
that

> everyone who, aroused by diabolical rage, strikes or does other injury to
> an image of the crucifix or to the nourishing Virgin [must], if they are
> laymen and nobles [pay] two hundred ducats, of which a fourth is for the
> Eight lords [of Security], a fourth for the accuser, a fourth for the
> presenting judge, and a fourth for the poor of Christ; if they are not nobles,
> it ordered that they should be bound by chains, dishonoured for three
> years by the hat [of infamy]; and if they are clerics, it desired that they
> should be deprived of their benefices, if they had any, [and] be suspended
> from the execution of their orders, and, if they had no benefices, be fined
> at the discretion of the bishop, suspended, and driven out in chains.[49]

pillory: ibid., XXVIII, cols. 1106–1107 and 1109.

   [47] See pp. 35–39 above.

   [48] V Lateran 1512–1517, *Sessio* X, 9, in *Conciliorum ... decreta* (n. 4 above), 621–622.
See *Dict. de droit can.* (n. 28 above), II, 914–915, and Leveleux, *Parole interdite* (n. 28
above), 82–84.

   [49] Mansi, *Collectio* (n. 16 above), XXXV, cols. 232–235. See R. Trexler, *Synodal
Law in Florence and Fiesole, 1307–1518*, Studi e testi 268 (Vatican City, 1971),
128–131; and idem, "Florentine Religious Experience: The Sacred Image" (1972),
repr. in his *Church and Community, 1200–1600: Studies in the History of Florence and
New Spain* (Rome, 1987), 51.

This decree was enacted only sixteen years after the execution of Rinaldeschi and by a group of churchmen of whom many must have been familiar with his case. The punishments they prescribed for striking and injuring an image of the Virgin were severe, but a long way from hanging.

This decree reflects the rising concern about blasphemy in the form of iconoclasm—the destruction and damage of images. Two cases in Pisa and Mantua concerned Jews who, albeit with ecclesiastical permission, destroyed two images respectively of St. Christopher and of the Virgin and Child.[50] The punishment was sometimes miraculous, as when a gambler in Gaeta who attacked a figure of St. Anthony after losing at play was simultaneously struck with the affliction known as St. Anthony's fire (ergotism) and died three days later.[51] Persons suspected of sacrilege were occasionally lynched by people who took the law into their own hands and meted out punishment with no regard for due process by contemporary standards. A Jew (called a *marrano*) was stoned to death in Florence in 1493, according to Landucci, because

> out of disrespect for Christians or more likely out of madness, he went about Florence marring images of Our Lady, and among others that which is of marble on the pillar outside Orsanmichele. He scratched the eye of the child and of St. Onophrius [and] threw dung at the face of Our Lady.[52]

---

[50] M. Luzzati, "Ebrei, Chiesa locale, 'Principe' e Popolo: due episodi di distruzione di immagini sacre alla fine del Quattrocento," in his *La casa dell'ebreo* (Pisa, 1985), 205–234, trans. in *Microhistory and the Lost Peoples of Europe*, ed. E. Muir and G. Ruggiero, trans. E. Branch (Baltimore, 1991), 101–118. On the desecration of holy images by Jews and others, see G. Jaritz, "The Destruction of Things in the Late Middle Ages," in *Emotions and Material Culture. International Round Table Discussion. Krems an der Donau, October 7 and 8, 2002* (Vienna, 2003), 67 and 73, pl. 4.

[51] Paolo di Tommaso Montauri, *Cronica senese*, in *Croniche senesi*, ed. A. Lisini and F. Iacometti, Rerum italicarum scriptores, 2nd ed., XV:6 (Bologna, 1939), 747. A pictorial example of the punishment of a man who threw stones at a statue of the Virgin is in the parallel cycles of the miracles of the Virgin in the Eton College Chapel and the Lady Chapel in Winchester.

[52] Landucci, *Diario* (above, ch. 1 n. 8), 66. The episode is recounted in greater and more gruesome detail by Tribaldo de' Rossi, *Ricordanze*, in *Delizie degli eruditi toscani*, ed. I. di San Luigi, 25 vols. in 26 (Florence, 1770–1789), XXIII, 283–285. On the episode and the offended statue of the Virgin see also D. F. Zervas, *Orsanmichele a Firenze*, 2 vols. (Modena, 1996), I, 220–221 and 460.

When the Florentine Captain in Pistoia refused to co-operate with some local vigilantes in 1502, they took it upon themselves to hang a gambler who had attacked a crucifix with a spike.[53] The following year in Florence Simone di Daniello del Pie was judicially hanged, according to the records of the Company of the Blacks, "for having burned and shamefully thrown into an enclosure an image of the crucifix and of Our Lady."[54]

This evidence shows that although there were no laws specifically punishing blasphemy with death aside from the Roman law tradition, which the Eight did not cite when condemning Rinaldeschi, there were many less formal precedents for imposing the death penalty. Rinaldeschi had offended "good morals" (*bonos mores*), and the Eight decided to act against him "in order that his punishment may be an example to others." In view of the number and severity of his offences, it is all the more striking that in his arrest and trial an effort was made to observe the form of the law, and that the scenes in the Stibbert painting seem to present the government itself as the chosen agent of a divine justice that might have worked through other avenues. This regard for the form of the law, combined with the severity of the punishment, needs to be understood in the light of the special circumstances in Florence at the end of the fifteenth and beginning of the sixteenth century.

---

[53] W. J. Connell, "Un cronista sconosciuto del primo '500: Bastiano Buoni e la sua cronica *De' casi di Pistoia*," *Bullettino storico pistoiese*, 95 (1993), 23–39 (35–36).
[54] Edgerton, *Pictures* (above, ch.1 n. 4), 55 n. 40.

CHAPTER 3
THE CONTEXT OF FLORENTINE HISTORY

Antonio Rinaldeschi's execution in the summer of 1501 took place during a delicate period of uncertainty and transition for the restored republican regime that was established seven years earlier, in 1494, with the exile of the Medici family. A crucial role in creating the regime had been played by the Dominican friar from Ferrara, Fra Girolamo Savonarola [Figure 20].[1] Beginning in the mid-1480s Savonarola had preached an apocalyptic message, to the effect that the church would be scourged and reformed, in the cities and towns of northern Italy. In 1490, at the invitation of Lorenzo de' Medici the Magnificent, the unofficial ruler of Florence, Savonarola was installed as reader in the Dominican convent of San Marco, where, by 1493, with the assistance of the Medici-controlled government, he created an observant congregation. Observantism, a movement that was common to most monastic orders in the fifteenth century, advocated stricter rules of discipline and a return to the intentions of each order's founder.

Savonarola claimed to be inspired by a revelation that the scourging and reform of Italy and the church would result from an invasion by a mighty king who would bring divine punishment on the sinful cities of

---

[1] On Savonarola see L. Polizzotto, *The Elect Nation: The Savonarolan Movement in Florence, 1494–1545* (Oxford, 1994); D. Weinstein, *Savonarola and Florence: Prophecy and Patriotism in the Renaissance* (Princeton, 1970); R. Ridolfi, *The Life of Girolamo Savonarola*, trans. C. Grayson (Westport, Conn., 1976); F. Cordero, *Savonarola*, 4 vols. (Bari, 1986–1988); *Savonarole: enjeux, débats, questions: actes du colloque international (Paris, 25–26–27 janvier 1996)*, ed. A. Fontes, J.-L. Fournel and M. Plaisance (Paris, 1996). The anniversary of Savonarola's death in 1998 resulted in an outpouring of publications, including *Girolamo Savonarola, l'uomo e il frate. Atti del XXXV Convegno storico internazionale, Todi, 11–14 ottobre 1998* (Spoleto, 1999); *The World of Savonarola: Italian Elites and Perceptions of Crisis*, ed. S. Fletcher and C. Shaw (Aldershot, 2000); and the many volumes in the series "Savonarola e la Toscana" published by SISMEL. For collections in English of Savonarola's work, see Girolamo Savonarola, *A Guide to Righteous Living and Other Works*, trans. K. Eisenbichler (Toronto, 2003); and the forthcoming *Selected Writings of Girolamo Savonarola: Religion and Politics, 1490–1498*, ed. D. Beebe, A. Borelli and M. Passaro.

Italy, and the invasion of Italy by Charles VIII of France in 1494 seemed resoundingly to confirm this message. With the exile of Piero de' Medici, Lorenzo de' Medici's son and heir, and the other members of the Medici family, Florence renewed its republican government, and Savonarola, through his preaching, encouraged the Florentines to establish a broadly based, *popolare* regime, that gave authority to a Great Council comprised of approximately 3000 citizens. As a spell-binding preacher who claimed access to divine revelation, Savonarola commanded a large following. Florence, he proclaimed, would lead the way to a reform of the Christian faith, from which the city would benefit both spiritually and materially. For the next several years Savonarola and his followers organized campaigns of moral renewal. Preaching that called for stricter laws against gambling, prostitution, blasphemy and homosexuality, and for the expulsion of Jews, was accompanied by public prayer, processions and bonfires of "vanities," in which licentious paintings and books, mirrors, luxurious clothing and jewellery were heaped in public squares and burned. Even Carnival was abolished in Florence, as Savonarola proclaimed a double period of Lent that included Carnival.

Not all of Florence went along with Savonarola's program. Opposed were many patricians and former Mediceans.[2] Savonarola's recommendations did not always become law, and preachers from other orders, particularly the Franciscans and the Servites, contested his claims. Most importantly, Savonarola came into conflict with Pope Alexander VI, who summoned him to Rome for examination. When Savonarola refused to obey and the Florentine government refused to yield him up, the Pope excommunicated the friar and threatened the city with interdict. In the spring of 1498, after Savonarola lost the support of the Florentine government, he and two of his Dominican followers were arrested and compelled under torture to confess to charges that included false prophesy. On 23 May 1498 the three men were hanged to death and their bodies were burned in the Piazza of the Signoria, which had previously been a site of Savonarola's bonfires of vanities [Figure 21].

The execution of Savonarola was a triumph for a group of patricians variously known to contemporaries as the *grandi* or *ottimati*. In the years

---

[2] One opponent was Niccolò Machiavelli, who spied on Savonarola's preaching and sent a highly critical report to a Florentine in Rome in a letter dated 9 March 1498, in *Machiavelli and His Friends: Their Personal Correspondence*, trans. and ed. J. B. Atkinson and D. Sices (DeKalb, Ill., 1996), 8–10.

that followed, however, the position of the *grandi* became progressively weaker in Florence as a consequence of their fumbling relations with France and their failures in the war to retake Pisa. In the winter and spring of 1501 the *grandi* seem to have become more desperate in their desire to reform the popular constitution, centred about the Great Council, which they hoped to abolish. In May 1501, when Cesare Borgia appeared with an army in Florentine territory and camped just north of the city, among his demands was the creation of a government of the few. It was widely assumed that Borgia had come at the invitation of the *grandi*. When Borgia was paid off by the popular government, leaving the Florentine dominion in June 1501, the *grandi* were discredited, and many of them withdrew from state affairs. There began a brief period of *popolare* and Savonarolan resurgence that historians in Florence have tended to overlook: indeed, in the year between June 1501 and June 1502, which was when Rinaldeschi committed his crime, Florence experienced its most thoroughly democratic regime since the revolt of the Ciompi in 1378.

In taking charge of Florentine affairs in 1501, the *popolari* were led by Piero Soderini.[3] Prior to 1500 Soderini appears to have taken little active role in domestic politics, serving instead on frequent missions abroad. Piero's older brother, Paolantonio, who was thought to favour a more oligarchic regime, determined the direction of the Soderini family in Florentine politics, and it seems clear from the record book kept by a third Soderini brother, Giovanvittorio, that the Soderini acted in concert

---

[3] A fierce historians' polemic surrounds the career of Piero Soderini. On the one hand, Roslyn Pesman Cooper and Humfrey Butters have read Soderini's actions as those of a fair-minded constitutionalist; on the other, Sergio Bertelli has portrayed Soderini as an ambitious politician who contemplated the establishment of a principate in Florence. See R. Pesman Cooper, "L'elezione di Pier Soderini a gonfaloniere a vita," *Archivio storico italiano*, 125 (1967), 145–185; S. Bertelli, "Petrus Soderinus Patriae Parens," *Bibliothèque d'humanisme et renaissance*, 31 (1969), 93–114; idem, "Pier Soderini, 'Vexillifer perpetuus reipublicae Florentinae,'" in *Renaissance Studies in Honor of Hans Baron*, ed. A. Molho and J.A. Tedeschi (DeKalb, Ill., 1971), 333–359; R. Pesman Cooper, "Pier Soderini: Aspiring Prince or Civic Leader," *Studies in Medieval and Renaissance History*, n.s., 1 (1978), 71–126; S. Bertelli, "'Uno magistrato per a tempo lungho o uno dogie'," in *Studi di storia medievale e moderna per Ernesto Sestan*, 2 vols. (Florence, 1980), II: 451–494; H. Butters, *Governors and Government in Early Sixteenth-Century Florence, 1502–1519* (Oxford, 1985); and S. Bertelli, "Di due profili mancati e di un bilancino con pesi truccati," *Archivio storico italiano*, 145 (1987), 579–610. Cooper's essays are now collected in her volume, *Pier Soderini and the Ruling Class in Renaissance Florence*, Bibliotheca Eruditorum 31 (Goldbach, 2002).

in these years.[4] With the death of Paolantonio in the summer 1499, leadership of the family passed to Piero, who in the winter of 1500–1501 deserted or was deserted by the *ottimati*, and as a consequence he began to support the institutions of the popular regime. In January and February 1501, when the *grandi* held a number of meetings to discuss proposals for narrowing the regime by curbing the Great Council, Soderini refused to attend. This became widely known, and it won him the favour of the *popolo*.[5] Soderini was elected to a two-month term as Standard Bearer of Justice for March–April 1501, and during his term he made a point of excluding the *grandi* from the deliberative meetings of the regime. Then, in the period of popular dominance that followed Borgia's failed invasion, Soderini played a leading part in government,[6] ultimately rescuing the regime by securing the support of the French king after the revolt of Arezzo and Valdichiana in 1502.[7]

Legislation was passed in 1501 that bolstered the regime's popular character. It was made easier to elect ambassadors and commissioners, now that the *grandi* were refusing such posts.[8] The number of Florentine offices to be filled through lot or sortition was increased.[9] In order to

---

[4] On Paolantonio's oligarchic tendencies, see Francesco Guicciardini, *Storie fiorentine dal 1378 al 1509*, ed. R. Palmarocchi (Bari, 1931), 183, who wrote of Paolantonio: ". . . era tenuto ambizioso, e che disiderassi mutare el governo e ristrignere lo stato in pochi cittadini." [. . . it was thought that he was ambitious, and that he wished to change the government and restrict the state to a few citizens.] The concerted political activity of the Soderini (Piero, Francesco, Giovanvittorio, and Tommaso the son of Paolantonio) is documented in Bertelli, "Uno magistrato" (n. 3 above), 475–478; and Bertelli, "Di due profili mancati" (n. 3 above), 582–589.

[5] Niccolò Machiavelli, *Legazioni. Commissarie. Scritti di governo*, ed. F. Chiappelli, 4 vols. (Bari, 1971–1985), I, 579; Guicciardini, *Storie fiorentine* (n. 4 above), 209.

[6] One indication of this prominence was the election on 20 January 1502 of Piero's nephew, Tommaso, as Florentine ambassador to the wedding of Lucrezia Borgia and Alfonso d'Este in Ferrara, recorded in Biagio Buonaccorsi, *Sunmario*, published in Machiavelli, *Legazioni* (n. 5 above), II, 570.

[7] That Soderini was seen as a hero is especially clear in a Latin letter, dated 14 September 1502, possibly written by Antonio di Bartolomeo Scala, to a fellow Florentine traveling in the eastern Mediterranean, which recounts the revolt of Arezzo and its suppression, published in *Annales Arretinorum maiores et minores*, ed. A. Bini and G. Grazzini, Rerum italicarum scriptores, 2nd ed., XXIV:1 (Città di Castello, 1909), 210–211.

[8] ASF, PR, 192, fols. 31^r–2^r (23 September 1501).

[9] ASF, PR, 192, fols. 15^v–16^v (30 July 1501), reduced the terms of office of several castellanies from one year to six months "[per] fare parte d'alchuni vostri uffici a più

make the Great Council more effective and stem an erosion of power toward the executive magistracies, an important measure reduced the size of the quorum necessary to approve laws to only 600 men.[10] The government even tried optimistically to impose a *popolare* regime in Pistoia, long controlled by rival magnate families, as a hoped-for antidote to endemic factionalism.[11] And in September 1501 the Great Council allowed Florence's powerful and elite war magistracy, the Ten of Liberty and Peace (*Dieci di libertà e pace*)—on which many of the *grandi* were accustomed to sit by virtue of their experience in affairs of state—to lapse, leaving military affairs to be managed by the Priors of the Signoria, who were chosen by lot.[12] The following year, as we have seen, the offices of the Podestà and Captain of the People were abolished and criminal jurisdiction was concentrated in the Eight for Security. It would be difficult not to read the Rinaldeschi episode in the light of this political change. Most importantly, as the *popolari* in Florence showed new strength, it was perhaps inevitable that the religious anxieties of the Savonarolan period from 1494 to 1498 should again find public expression.

To be sure, some Florentines seem to have been looking for ways to emphasize moments in the city's religious past that were not specifically linked to the Dominican friar. Thus in December 1500 the Great

---

numero di cittadini." [. . . to open some of your offices to a greater number of citizens.]

[10] As reported in Landucci, *Diario* (above, ch. 1 n. 8), 235 (4 August 1501).

[11] This was the stated aim of two plans (*Sommarii*) for Pistoia composed in March 1502. Mistakenly attributed to Machiavelli, who did write a brief account *On Pistoiese Affairs* (*De rebus pistoriensibus*) at this time, they were published in Niccolò Machiavelli, *Tutte le opere*, ed. M. Martelli, (Florence, 1971), 6–8. J.-J. Marchand, *Niccolò Machiavelli. I primi scritti politici (1499–1512)*, Medioevo e umanesimo 23 (Padua, 1975), 45 n. 9, and 48 n. 18, rejected the attribution. See also W. J. Connell, *La città dei crucci: fazioni e clientele in uno stato repubblicano del '400* (Florence, 2000), 222.

[12] Twice the Great Council allowed the magistracy of the Ten to lapse in these years, first for the period May 1499–September 1500, and again for the period September 1501–June 1502. (For the first reestablishment of the Ten, see ASF, PR, 191, fols. 27^r–28^r [18 September 1500]; and for their second reestablishment, in 1502, see *Annales Arretinorum* [n. 7 above], 179). The fact that there was no committee of experienced citizens in charge of military affairs during these years was one of Machiavelli's chief criticisms of the Florentine popular regime, expressed in his *Discourses on Livy*, I, 39, in Machiavelli, *Tutte le opere*, ed. Martelli (n. 11 above), 122–123. In an influential study F. Gilbert, *Machiavelli and Guicciardini: Politics and History in Sixteenth-Century Florence*, 2nd ed. (New York, 1984), 61–62 and 169, misread the historical evidence concerning the authority of the Ten, and accused Machiavelli, wrongly in this instance, of "designing examples to fit his purposes."

Council voted to celebrate the feast day (12 July) of the eleventh-century Florentine saint John Gualbert as an annual civic holiday.[13] In April 1502 it was decided to make Gualbert's feast day even more important by celebrating it in the same manner as the feast of St. Francis.[14] St. Francis, too, became the focus of special attention, not only because the Franciscans had consistently opposed and finally triumphed over Savonarola's Dominicans in 1498, but also because Franciscanism offered an alternative tradition of popular piety with ancient and impeccable credentials. Piero Soderini seems to have made a pilgrimage to the Franciscan monastery at La Verna, also in 1502, in the period between his election as Florence's first and only Standard-Bearer of Justice for Life (*Gonfaloniere di giustizia a vita*) and his assumption of office.[15] And in 1503 the commissioner general Antonio Giacomini sent St. Francis's cloak, seized as a war trophy in Citerna, to Florence, where it was displayed in the convent of the observant Franciscans, S. Francesco al Monte alle Croci (now called S. Salvatore al Monte), located above the city near the very old church of San Miniato.[16] From 1498 through the early 1500s the architect Cronaca directed a massive building program at this Franciscan convent, which, according to Lorenzo Polizzotto, functioned as "headquarters of the

---

13 ASF, PR, 191, fol. 59[r–v] (17–20 December 1500), which reads in part: ". . . essendo stato detto Giovanni Gualberto di natione fiorentina et molto divoto per la sua sanctità et frequentia de' miracoli per lui in diversi tempi dimonstrati. . . ." [. . . since said John Gualbert was a Florentine by birth and very holy on account of his sanctity and the frequency of the miracles revealed by him at various times. . . .]

14 ASF, PR, 193, fols. 16[v]–17[v] (19 April 1502).

15 Letter from the Ten of Liberty and Peace to Piero Soderini, copy in ASF, Dieci di balìa. Carteggi. Missive interne, 70, fol. 139[r] (26 September 1502): ". . . perché tu mostri desiderare di intendere se e' ci piacerebbe che ti trasferissi a La Vernia [*sic*], ti rispondiamo come e' ci è grato ogni tua commodità." [. . . since you show that you wish to know if it would please us for you to go to La Verna, we reply that your every convenience pleases us.]

16 Letter from Antonio Giacomini to the Ten of Liberty and Peace, original in ASF, Dieci di balìa. Carteggi. Responsive, 66, fol. 230[r] (29 January 1502/3): "Magnifici domini etc. Io mi serbai la chiave della cassa dove è l'abito di san Francesco et del forzerino dell'altre reliquie che è in decta cassa et suggellai in sulla serratura a fine che fussi prima vista costì che a nissun altra parte. . . ." [Magnificent lords, etc. I have kept the key to the chest that contains the habit of St. Francis and to the small strongbox with the other relics that is in said chest, and I have put a seal on the lock so that it may be seen there [in Florence] first, before anywhere else. . . .] For the cloak's arrival in Florence, see Landucci, *Diario* (above, ch. 1 n. 8), 253.

recently victorious campaign against Savonarola."[17] Rinaldeschi was arrested in the garden of this very convent [Figure 4], which overlooked Florence, after his act of sacrilege.

Yet Savonarola was still on the minds of many Florentines. By 1501 much of the Florentine populace had come to consider the Ferrarese friar a holy man martyred for political reasons. There was concern that if Savonarola, who had made Christ "King of Florence," had been holy, then the entire city had been an accomplice in his death. This was the message of a peasant from Brozzi called Martino who in the winter of 1500–1501 harangued the passersby, proclaiming himself the friar's successor and prophesying that God would punish Italy and the cities of Rome and Florence for having killed Savonarola and his two followers in 1498.[18]

Certainly the Rinaldeschi episode of 1501 deserves to be interpreted with a view to this background of religious feeling. Condemnations of gambling and blasphemy were a staple of Savonarola's preaching, leading to stricter legislation and enforcement.[19] A quantitative study of one class of offence, Florentine convictions for sodomy—a moral crime of which Rinaldeschi was not accused, but which Savonarola took quite seriously—has shown that although these declined for more than two years after the friar's death, they again soared during the period from November 1500 to November 1502, when the Rinaldeschi episode also occurred.[20]

One of the more striking qualities of the Savonarola movement was its attempt to seek control over streets and street-corners in Florence, such as the one that became the scene of Rinaldeschi's crime. The historian Piero Parenti relates that during the Savonarola's Lenten "Carnival" of 1496, "small altars and crucifixes and other figures" were placed "at almost every street-corner."[21] Savonarola's concern with local devotion was combined with a forceful and consistent message concerning visual images. His campaign against secular representations resulted in a heightened awareness among his followers toward all images, whether

---

[17]Polizzotto, *Elect Nation* (n. 1 above), 170. See also 208.

[18]Giovanni Cambi, *Istorie*, in *Delizie* (above, ch. 2 n. 52), XXI:168.

[19]See Rizzi, *Ludus* (above, ch. 2 n. 3), 111 and 129–130, and, generally, the references in ch. 2 n. 13 above.

[20]M. Rocke, *Forbidden Friendships: Homosexuality and Male Culture in Renaissance Florence* (New York, 1996), 224.

[21]Piero di Marco Parenti, *Storia fiorentina*, ed. A. Matucci, I (Florence, 1994), 311.

religious or profane.[22] More specifically, he preached against expensive contemporary religious images that "eclipse[d] the light of God," and in favour of older images of the kind that Rinaldeschi offended.[23] The reaction to his sacrilege reflected a sense of outrage at the dishonour to the Virgin in a city that, through measures like the rededication of the Cathedral to her in 1412, had developed its own political Mariology.[24] But the response may also have been provoked by a more immediate fear that owing to its sins, including the execution of Savonarola and his two followers, Florence no longer enjoyed divine favour and protection.[25] The fact that Rinaldeschi fled to the anti-Savonarolan convent of the observant Franciscans, where he possibly hoped for protection, may indicate that the criminal himself was aware of Savonarolan motives for the manhunt that led to his death.

Through the creation and development of a devotion to the Madonna de' Ricci immediately after Rinaldeschi's death, the continuing Savonarolan impulses in Florence found a specific and enduring focus. The membership of the *opera* that was formed to protect and honour the image Rinaldeschi defiled makes this strikingly clear. According to a document published by Richa in his history of the church of S. Maria degli Alberighi, the parishioners first elected five directors (*hoperai*) on 26 July 1501, and among their number was Piero di Bernardo Adimari, who was not only a relative of the archbishop's vicar, but also a signer of an important 1497 petition of the citizenry on behalf of Savonarola.[26] When

---

[22] H. Bredekamp, "Renaissancekultur als 'Hölle': Savonarolas Verbrennungen der Eitelkeiten," in *Bildersturm* (above, Foreword n. 6), 41–64, likened it to a fetishism.

[23] Girolamo Savonarola, *Prediche italiane ai Fiorentini*, ed. F. Cognasso and R. Palmarocchi, 3 vols. in 4 (Perugia-Venice-Florence, 1930–1935), II: 161–162 (17 May 1495), cited also by Belting, *Likeness* (above, Foreword n. 7), 72.

[24] M. Bergstein, "Marian Politics in Quattrocento Florence: The Renewed Dedication of Santa Maria del Fiore in 1412," *Renaissance Quarterly*, 44 (1991), 673–719.

[25] Such feelings are particularly pronounced in periods of radical change, when old values and attitudes are challenged. For a parallel in very different circumstances, see J. M. Merriman, "Incident at the Statue of the Virgin Mary: The Conflict of Old and New in Nineteenth-Century Limoges," in *Consciousness and Class Experience in Nineteenth-Century Europe*, ed. J.M. Merriman (New York-London, 1979), 129–148, who studied in particular the fierce devotion of the butchers in Limoges in the late nineteenth and early twentieth century to "their" statue of the Virgin.

[26] Richa, *Notizie* (above, ch. 1 n.4), VIII, 243–247; Polizzotto, *Elect Nation* (n. 1 above), 446. For the election of the first *operai* see also ASF, NA, 7981, Ser Francesco da Romena, no. 149 (26 July 1501); and Banc., MSS, 54, fol. 131 [left] (26 July 1501).

four additional rectors were elected on 18 September, these included the prominent Savonarolan Bartolomeo Pandolfini, who was also a signer of the 1497 petition, and who was later banned from public office for criticizing Medici policy.[27] By 2 September 1507, when another document listed the *operai*, who now numbered eleven, two of the city's most prominent supporters of Savonarola had joined the committee: Francesco di Filippo del Pugliese and Girolamo Benivieni, each of whom was banned from public office for two years in 1498 after the friar's death, and who continued actively to keep his memory alive for decades.[28] Apart from these four known followers of the friar, most of the other directors of the *opera* served for obviously practical reasons, since they included the rector of the church, a former rector, a parishioner whose house was demolished by the oratory, and two members of the Ricci family, whose ancestor had originally commissioned the tabernacle. The continuing devotion to the Virgin offended by Rinaldeschi offered a way of furthering in Florence many of the religious sentiments that characterized the Savonarolan movement, while the devotion's *opera* and the oratory it constructed provided a means for Savonarola's many adherents to continue to congregate after his death, notwithstanding official condemnations of the friar's teachings, and attempts by the ruling Medici family, after their return to Florence in 1512, to root out the Savonarolism that persisted in other religious contexts, including the Dominican convent of San Marco.[29] In 1533 one patrician follower of Savonarola, Jacopo

---

[27] ASF, NA, 7981, Ser Francesco da Romena, no. 152 (18 September 1501); Banc. MSS, 54, fol. 132^v (18 September 1501). Cf. Polizzotto, *Elect Nation* (n. 1 above), 274, 456.

[28] ASF, NA, 7981, Ser Francesco da Romena, no. 195 (2 September 1507), which appears below in the Appendix as Document IX. On Pugliese, see Polizzotto, *Elect Nation* (n. 1 above), 263–264. On Benivieni, see C. Re, *Girolamo Benivieni fiorentino* (Città di Castello, 1906); Polizzotto, *Elect Nation* (n. 1 above), 141–146, 166–168 and passim; and O. Zorzi Pugliese, "Girolamo Benivieni seguace e difensore del Savonarola," in *Studi savonaroliani. Verso il V centenario*, ed. G. C. Garfagnini (Florence, 1996), 309–318.

[29] On the continuing part played by the memory of Savonarola in Florentine politics and society, and on the condemnation of his teachings by Florentine authorities, see Polizzotto, *Elect Nation* (n. 1 above), 239–445; M. Firpo, *Gli affreschi di Pontormo a San Lorenzo. Eresia, politica e cultura nella Firenze di Cosimo I* (Turin, 1997), 341–344; and A. Matucci, "L'abiura di don Teodoro: divertimento novellistico o calcolo politico," in *Storiografia repubblicana fiorentina (1494–1570)*, ed. J.-J. Marchand and J.-C. Zancarini (Florence, 2003), 197–207.

Salviati, established and endowed, together with his wife Lucrezia (a daughter of Lorenzo de' Medici the Magnificent), two chapels in the oratory of the Madonna de' Ricci. The Savonarolan Girolamo Benivieni continued to play an active role in the administration of the oratory of the Madonna de' Ricci down to his death in 1542, when he was succeeded by a nephew, Michele, the son of the famous physician Antonio Benivieni who had been yet another well-known Savonarolan.[30]

How long the connection between Savonarolism and the Madonna de' Ricci persisted, and when it was forgotten, is difficult to know. Possibly it was owing to a continuing odour of Savonarolan unorthodoxy that the Madonna de' Ricci was omitted from an authoritative listing of Marian images throughout the world, the *Atlas Marianus*, which was published between 1655 and 1657 by the German Jesuit Wilhelm Gumppenberg.[31] In this regard it cannot have helped that the Florentine informants for Gumppenberg's survey were Servites from the nearby church of the Santissima Annunziata, which was home both to a rival Marian image and a tradition of anti-Savonarolism. In 1630, with the mediation of Grand Duke Ferdinand II, the *operai* of the Madonna de' Ricci ceded control of the oratory to the Scolopi Fathers, a new order with a mission in education. The Scolopi administered S. Maria degli Alberighi as a parish church until 1775, and perhaps it was in this period that the Savonarolism that once surrounded the image faded and was lost to memory.[32]

Yet it would be a mistake to read the devotion to the Madonna de' Ricci as a phenomenon that was simply Savonarolan. The esconcement of a group of the friars' devotees in a new oratory that they were permitted to build in the heart of Florence would not have happened had the circumstances surrounding Rinaldeschi's crime not corresponded exceptionally well with traditions concerning religious images and popular devotions that were widely accepted. There was a close connection

---

[30] Banc., MSS, 54, fol.139[r].

[31] *Atlante Mariano, ossia origine delle immagini miracolose della B.V. Maria venerate in tutte le parti del mondo*, compiled by W. Gumppenberg, ed. A. Zanella, 17 vols. (Verona, 1839–1847). On Gumppenberg, see G. Cracco, "Prospettive sui santuari. Dal secolo delle devozioni al secolo delle religioni," in *Per una storia* (above, Foreword n. 7), 7–61 (11–25). Gumppenberg's chief informants in Florence for his seventeenth-century survey were the Servites who had a tradition of anti-Savonarolism.

[32] The present parish priest, Roberto Tassi, who has written a history of the church (above, ch. 1 n. 3), is not aware of it.

between lay piety and images in fifteenth-century Italian cities,[33] and it is not surprising that a popular cult, accompanied by signs and miracles, began to develop around the image desecrated by Rinaldeschi almost as soon as, and perhaps before, his execution. Contemporary records of paintings that wept, bled, sweated, closed their eyes or changed colours were fairly common in northern Italy and indeed throughout Europe in the late fifteenth and early sixteenth centuries.[34] "The inherent efficacy of the tavola was clearly not distinguished from the efficacy of the crowd behavior," writes Richard Trexler, who studied in particular the importance of images of the Virgin. "Mary was the dynamic repository of power. She was where her image was being worshiped."[35] As Edward Muir writes, "Intercessors with the divine permeated urban spaces . . . to such a degree that rigid distinctions between sacred and profane . . . must have seemed alien, even irreligious, to many who lived in towns magically tied together by little shrines."[36] Other scholars have stressed the search

---

[33] E. Muir, "The Virgin on the Street Corner: The Place of the Sacred in Italian Cities," in *Religion and Culture in the Renaissance and Reformation*, ed. S. Ozment, Sixteenth Century Essays and Studies 11 (Kirksville, 1989), 25–40, esp. 30 on images, where he said that "popular practice tended. . . to create sacred places," and 34–37 on Florence.

[34] For a Virgin in Florence who in 1470 complained aloud, see Trexler, *Public Life* (above, ch. 1 n. 14), 114. For one who closed her eyes in 1506, see Landucci, *Diario* (above, ch. 1 n. 8), 279. In Florentine territory there were miraculous episodes involving paintings of the Madonna at Bibbona in 1482, Prato in 1484, Pistoia and Arezzo in 1490, Bagno di Romagna in 1498, and Montepulciano in 1514 and again in 1518. For Bibbona, see Landucci, *Diario* (above, ch. 1 n. 8), 41; for Prato, L. Bandini, "Il quinto centenario della 'mirabilissima apparitione,' " *Archivio storico pratese*, 60 (1984), 55–96; for Pistoia, *Centenario del miracolo della Madonna dell'Umiltà a Pistoia* (Pistoia, 1992); for Arezzo, D.A. Dragoni, *Antichità e ragguardevolezza della venerabil' Compagnia della Santissima Annunziata d'Arezzo e della sua chiesa altrimenti detta dipoi di Santa Maria delle lagrime* (Florence, 1759); for Bagno di Romagna and Montepulciano, G. Batini and E. Guarnieri, *Il pianto della Madonna* (Florence, 1995), 20 and 53–55. For a similar episode outside Naples, see M. Miele, *Le origini della Madonna dell'Arco. Il "Compendio" di Arcangelo Domenici* (Naples-Bari, 1995). In general on these phenomena, see M.P. Carroll, *Madonnas that Maim: Popular Catholicism in Italy since the Fifteenth Century* (Baltimore, 1992), esp. 52–87, on the Marian cult, which treats images of the Madonna as "dangerous" and their assailants as victims. See also W. A. Christian, Jr., *Apparitions in Late Medieval and Renaissance Spain* (Princeton, 1981); and idem, *Moving Crucifixes in Modern Spain* (Princeton, 1992), stressing the importance of political context in interpreting such occurrences.

[35] Trexler, "Florentine Religious Experience" (above, ch. 2 n. 49), 47, 55–56.

[36] Muir, "The Virgin" (n. 33 above), 25–26.

for "spiritual authentication," as it has been called, by the laity and also by the government, patriciate and church in Florence and "the transfer of the scene of religious ritual from reserved monastic or ecclesiastical space to public, civic space."[37]

Like the Madonna de' Ricci, many of the images that gave rise to popular devotions came to public notice after they were damaged or otherwise offended. Attacks on these paintings revealed a vulnerability that caused the faithful to endow the images with compensatory powers. The painting's weakness as a delicate artefact became a source of its strength.[38]

The fresco of the Virgin Annunciate that became the object of Rinaldeschi's crime was situated in a tabernacle commissioned in the mid-fourteenth century by Rosso de' Ricci. Originally, the tabernacle is said to have housed a painting by Giovanni da Milano, a pupil of Taddeo Gaddi.[39] Contemporary accounts stress that the tabernacle was neglected; nonetheless in the second half of the fifteenth century there was sufficient interest in the tabernacle to result in the original painting's being replaced by the fresco of the Annunciation in Renaissance style that is clearly visible in the Stibbert panel [Figure 25].

---

[37] M. Becker, "Aspects of Lay Piety in Early Renaissance Florence," in *The Pursuit of Holiness in Late Medieval and Renaissance Religion*, ed. C. Trinkaus and H. A. Oberman (Leiden, 1974), 181; D. Weinstein, "Critical Issues in the Study of Civic Religion in Renaissance Florence," ibid., 267; and D. Peterson, "Religion, Politics and the Church in Fifteenth-Century Florence," in *Girolamo Savonarola: Piety, Prophecy and Politics*, ed. D. Weinstein and V.R. Hotchkiss (Dallas, 1994), 75–84.

[38] D. Freedberg, *The Power of Images : Studies in the History and Theory of Response* (Chicago, 1991); *Macht und Ohnmacht* (above, Foreword n. 6); and *The Miraculous Image in the Late Middle Ages and Renaissance*, ed. E. Thunø and G. Wolf, Analecta Romana Instituti Danici, Supplementum 35 (Rome, 2004).

[39] Richa, *Notizie* (above, ch. 1 n. 4), VIII, 252; W. and E. Paatz, *Die Kirchen von Florenz. Ein kunstgeschichtliches Handbuch*, 6 vols. (Frankfurt am Main, 1940–1954), III, 97, 104. For the main façade of the church as it existed in the mid-fifteenth century see Figure 22, an illustration from the "Libro intitolato dell'andata o viaggio al S. Sepolcro al Monte Sinai compilato da Marco di Bartolommeo Rustici orafo di Firenze l'anno 1425," reproduced in A. Sapori, *Compagnie e mercanti di Firenze antica* (Florence, 1955), LXXI, fig. 16 (repr. 1978, LXXVII, fig. 16). The side door above which the Ricci tabernacle stood is not visible. The foreground shows Mary, the church's eponymous saint, seated next to a spinning wheel and reading to the child Christ. Reproductions of this and other illustrations from the Rustici manuscript are also found in G. Fanelli, *Firenze architettura e città*, 2 vols. (Florence, 1973), II, 64–66, figs. 350–384. The manuscript dates from 1447 or shortly thereafter.

The precise date of the start of the cult associated with the Rinaldeschi incident is not clear, but the fact that the archbishop came to see the defiled image and that his vicar ordered it to be cleaned on the morning of the execution suggests that it had already attracted considerable attention.[40] One of the records of the Company of the Blacks for 22 July 1501 stated that "the devotion and thronging of persons began and ensued." Landucci recorded on 21 July 1501, the day of Rinaldeschi's trial and condemnation, that

> All Florence came to see, so that when the bishop came to see this Virgin Mary, he cleaned her of said dung, so that before evening came, many pounds of wax were hung there, as all the while the devotion grew. And in a few days a great many images [ex votos] were brought there, as shall be seen afterward.[41]

The "Narration of the crime of Rinaldeschi" in the book of the "Income, expense, debtors, creditors and memories" of the church of S. Maria degli Alberighi also says that on the morning of the execution the vicar of the archbishop of Florence ordered that the image be cleaned and that it soon became an object of popular veneration.

It was agreed on 26 July 1501, four days after Rinaldeschi's execution, that all the alms, wax and other gifts given to the image would be used by the opera to honour and adorn the image.[42] Plans to acquire and demolish houses near the church are evident in a notarial document dated 15 August;[43] and on 23 August 1501 the opera received permission from the "Officers of the Tower" (the Ufficiali della torre, who issued building permits) to build four pilasters in the piazza next to the church for a covered chapel running alongside the church.[44] The Eight for Security assigned part of Rinaldeschi's confiscated property to this purpose.[45] On 27 August the opera was granted permission to build gates

---

[40]The date of 13 July 1508, when a new oratory around the image began to be built (see below, p. 65), may have been the anniversary of the first appearance of the cult.

[41]Landucci, Diario (above, ch. 1 n. 8), 233–234, cf. tr. Jervis, 187–188; Lapini (above, ch. 1 n. 8), 44.

[42]Richa, Notizie (above, ch. 1 n. 4), VIII, 237; Banc., MSS, 54, fol. 1ʳ (26 July 1501).

[43]ASF, NA, 7981, Ser Francesco da Romena, no. 151 (15 August 1501).

[44]Richa, Notizie (above, ch. 1 n. 4), VIII, 237; Banc., MSS, 54, fol. 132ʳ (23 August 1501).

[45]Richa, Notizie (above, ch. 1 n. 4), VIII, 251, 255.

at the two entrances to the piazza neighbouring S. Maria degli Alberighi
so as to control access to the Madonna.[46] A chaplain was elected on 17
September and the next day four new members were elected to the *opera*
with all of the *operai* being confirmed for ten years and the chaplain for
one year.[47] Subsequent entries in the *opera*'s register at Berkeley, and
several notarial acts recording land transfers, detail the activities of the
operai as they proceeded with their plans for the oratory. Payment
records show that the roof was finished by 24 February 1502; and, since
the last entry in the construction account is dated 22 May 1502, it seems
reasonable to conclude that by then the building was complete.[48]

The original oratory had been built in haste, however, and with
the continued success of the new devotion, it was decided in 1507 to
construct a more splendid building in order to accommodate the
growing cult better. According to a notarial document dated 2 September 1507, the *operai* entrusted this task to the prominent architect, Baccio
d'Agnolo, on the basis of a wooden model they had previously requested.[49] Baccio's commission for the oratory of the Madonna de' Ricci
has not been known to architectural historians, but it was certainly a
prestigious one, since he was then at the height of his career. Since 1499
Baccio had been head of the office of works for the Palace of the
Signoria, where, among many projects, he designed a private apartment
for Piero Soderini. In 1506, he was one of four architects named to
direct the Cathedral works and to design the still unfinished gallery to
join the drum of the Cathedral with Brunelleschi's dome.[50] The terms

---

[46] Banc., MSS, 54, fol. 132ʳ (27 August 1501).

[47] Banc., MSS, 54, fol. 132ʳ⁻ᵛ (17–18 September 1501); ASF, NA, 7981, no. 152
(18 September 1501).

[48] Banc., MSS, 54, fols. 132ʳ–137ʳ, record the activities of the *opera* during this
period, while the expense accounts on fols. 20ᵛ–23ᵛ (26 July 1501 to 22 May 1502)
detail progress in constructing the oratory. Additional documents concerning the
property transactions of the *opera* may be found in ASF, NA, 16791, Ser Piero di
Andrea da Campi, fols. 35ᵛ–36ʳ (27 January 1501/2); NA, 9648, Ser Giovanni di
Marco da Romena, fols. 144ʳ⁻ᵛ, 145ʳ, 152ʳ–153ᵛ (all of 5 December 1502); NA, 9649,
Ser Giovanni di Marco da Romena, fols. 128ʳ–131ᵛ (28 November 1504).

[49] ASF, NA, 7981, Ser Francesco da Romena, no. 195 (2 September 1507),
published in the Appendix as Document IX.

[50] A. Cecchi, "Percorso di Baccio d'Agnolo legnaiuolo e architetto fiorentino,"
Antichità viva, 29, no.1 (1990), 31–46 and nos. 2–3 (1990), 40–55; C. Elam, "Baccio
d'Agnolo," in *The Dictionary of Art*, ed. J. Turner, 34 vols. (London, 1996), III, 15–17.
The commission has remained unknown for two reasons: it was not mentioned in

under which the *opera* of S. Maria degli Alberighi hired Baccio stated that he would receive three broad gold florins per month throughout the construction plus two broad gold florins as payment for his model, and that in his absence his associate Antonio da Sangallo (the Elder) would direct the work.

Construction began on 13 July 1508, when Landucci wrote in his diary that "On this day were begun the foundations of the Nunziata de' Ricci, which is called Santa Maria Alberighi, that which began from that man who threw filth in the face [of the Virgin] and who was hanged."[51] Regulations for the *operai* who lived next to the church were drawn up in 1508,[52] and the record of a pastoral visit to S. Maria degli Alberighi in January 1510 stated that the church was joined (*coniuncta est*) "to that image of the Annunciation for which there is very great veneration on account of the innumerable miracles and graces" and that there were twelve resident chaplains, of whom each received five pounds out of the oblations received by the four *operarii* who were responsible for admitting the devout.[53] On 23 October 1511 Landucci recorded that "The church of the Virgin Mary of Por San Piero was furnished with a covering, that is, the main body of the church."[54]

The outline of Baccio d'Agnolo's oratory can be made out alongside S. Maria degli Alberighi in Stefano Buonsignori's 1585 map of Florence [Figure 23].[55] Like the first oratory of 1502, however, his structure fell victim to its own success, since the site was further transformed as the devotion to the Madonna de' Ricci continued to grow. A new altar was established in the oratory in 1523;[56] and sometime between 1585 and

---

early published sources, including Vasari's life of Baccio, and the oratory itself no longer survives.

[51] Landucci, *Diario* (above, ch. 1 n. 8), 287: "E in questi dì si cominciò e fondamenti della Nunziata de' Ricci, che si dice Santa Maria Alberighi, quella che si cominciò da quello che gli gittò nel viso bruttura e fu inpiccato." The date "1503" in Torricelli, *Madonna de' Ricci* (above, ch.1 n. 4), 11, is a typographical error, as becomes clear on 15.

[52] Richa, *Notizie* (above, ch. 1 n. 4), VIII, 243–247.

[53] Florence, Archivio della Curia arcivescovile, Visite pastorali, VP03, fasc. 6, unpaginated.

[54] Landucci, *Diario* (above, ch. 1 n. 8), 311.

[55] Stefano Buonsignori, *Nova pulcherrimae civitatis Florentiae topographia accuratissime delineata* (Florence, 1584). For a reproduction of the entire map, which was executed for Grand Duke Francesco de' Medici, see Fanelli, *Firenze* (n. 39 above), II, 110–111, figs. 600–601.

1616, a new façade was built for S. Maria degli Alberighi. In the seventeenth century the oratory and the church came to be administered jointly as the Church of the Madonna de' Ricci. The present façade on the Via del Corso [Figure 24] was built in 1640–1641, and it includes in its portico the coat-of-arms of the Eight for Security.[57] There were further building campaigns in 1709 and 1769,[58] and on 8 May 1771, in a solemn ceremony, the fresco of the Madonna de' Ricci was cut from her old place on what had become an interior side wall and transferred to a position above the main altar, where she floats today surrounded by gilded cherubim [Figures 26–27].[59]

Some interesting additional light is thrown on these developments by the records of a case tried in the archiepiscopal court in 1545 between S. Maria degli Alberighi and a smith named Giovanni di Simone, who had a workshop of which the noise disturbed the services in the church. The church's procurator claimed, with lawyerly circumlocution, that

> The image of the holy Virgin that makes signs and images and is in the oratory built next to the old church of S. Maria degli Alberighi both was and is very old, and a hundred and more years have already elapsed, enough and more so that there was and is no memory what its beginning was, and it is and was on the old wall of the said S. Maria degli Alberighi, and so it was also before the existing oratory was made there in honour of the image of the holy Virgin.[60]

---

56 Richa, *Notizie* (above, ch. 1 n. 4),VIII, 252.

57 L. Botteri, "Novità sulla Madonna de' Ricci: la facciata," *Rivista d'arte*, 38 (1986), 87–113; and O. Tosti, "Il portico di S. Maria de' Ricci. Notizie storiche," *Ricerche. Bollettino degli Scolopi italiani*, 13 (1993), 353–361.

58 Paatz and Paatz, *Die Kirchen* (n. 39 above), III, 93.

59 The transferral of the fresco was discussed in a printed flier, *Relazione della miracolosa immagine della SS. Annunziata che si venera in Firenze nella chiesa della Madonna de' Ricci* (Florence, 1773), 4, reprinted in Tassi, *Chiesa Madonna de' Ricci* (above, ch. 1 n. 3), 372, which also retold the story of Rinaldeschi much as it appeared in the earlier flier of 1718, cited above (ch. 1 n. 3).

60 Florence, Archivio della Curia arcivescovile, Cause civili, Chiese determinate, CD364.3, insert of "Acta in causa ecclesie S. Marie de Alberigis contra Ioannem Simonis Fabrum," unpaginated (5 September 1545): ". . . quod imago dive Virginis faciens signa et miracula et existens in oratorio fabricato prope dictam veterem ecclesiam Sancte Marie de Alberigis fuit et est etiam antiquissima, et iam sunt centum anni elapsi et satis ultra et tanto tempore cuius initii non est memoria quod fuit et est et erat in muro veteri dicte Sancte Marie de Alberigis, et sic etiam antequam fieret oratorium ibi existens ad honorem dicte imaginis dive Virginis."

Then, turning to the history of the oratory, the procurator said

> that forty years and more had elapsed since the existing oratory in honour
> of the said image was built, next to and connected to the said old church
> and to its wall where the said image is, owing to the miracles and signs
> which it worked, and to the throngs and devotion of the faithful.[61]

It was also forty years since daily masses began to be celebrated in the
oratory on the altar before the image. Before the oratory was built, (still
according to the procurator for the church), there was an alley with no
shops in it, but now the noise of hammering from Giovanni's smithy
"greatly impeded the celebration and hearing of the masses and other
holy offices."[62]

The procurator for Giovanni, in presenting his case, added some
important details, including that the oratory was called the "oratorio del
Rinaldescho," that in 1501 "an image of the most glorious Virgin Mary
decorated [the] outside [of the] church of S. Maria degli Alberighi of
Florence and made a public sign (signum publicum)," and that long before
that time there had been smithies and other workshops in the street.[63]

The court set seven questions to be asked of established inhabitants
in the area surrounding the church. Among these was "Whether they
knew that Filippo Dolciati painted and made the image of the Virgin
Mary next to the said church and that he decorated the Virgin in this
way in the year 1501 [Florentine style] and that it was about thirty years
since the said oratory was built."[64] In the subsequent interrogations
Giovan Battista de' Mini said that he did not know whether Filippo
Dolciati painted the image of the Virgin and "that the truth is that in
the year 1501 it was said that the said image of the Virgin Mary showed

---

[61] Ibid., ". . . quod iam sunt elapsi 40 anni et ultra quod fabricatum fuit oratorium
ibi existens ad honorem dicte imaginis contiguum et connexum dicte ecclesie veteris
et eius muro ubi est dicta imago propter miracula et signa que faciebat et propter
concursum et devotionem fidelium."

[62] Ibid., ". . . propter magnum strepitum et fragorem immissum in dictam ecclesiam sive oratorium impedit summopere celebrationem et auditionem missarum et
aliorum divinorum. . . ."

[63] Ibid. (30 May 1545): "de anno 1501 . . . inmago gloriosissime Virginis Marie extra
ecclesiam Sancte Marie de Alberigis de Florentia decoravit et signum publicum fecit."

[64] Ibid., "Item. Si sciunt quod Filippus Dolciati pinxit et fecit imaginem Virginis
Marie iuxta dictam ecclesiam et quod de anno 1501 huiusmodi Virginem decoravit
et quod iam sunt anni 30 in circa quod fuit fabbricatum oratorium predictum."

a miracle, which was well known, and that the truth is that the said new oratory was not built until about four years after the said miracle."[65] Another witness also testified that the miracle associated with the image took place in or about 1501;[66] and another, Niccolò di Baldo, said that the church was decorated "on account of the miracle which appeared on or about 1501 because a certain . . . Rinaldeschi was hanged on account of his offences (*demerita*)."[67]

None of these sources, nor those associated directly with Rinaldeschi's case, specified the nature of the miracle. The records of the *opera* suggest three possibilities. The first, and most explicit, is that a small amount of the dung thrown at the image by Rinaldeschi "miraculously (*miracholosamente*) . . . remained stuck in the diadem above the nape of her neck, so that it almost resembled a dry rosette."[68] The version of this account published by Richa added the words "such as one still sees" and also, after the subsequent reference to the cleaning of the image at the order of the archbishop's vicar, "but the sign remains." This suggests that the account was revised when it was copied from the *opera* register, probably in 1508, in order to emphasize the survival of the miraculous rosette, which was either spared during the cleaning, or subsequently restored and gilded, perhaps as part of the work done by the painter Filippo Dolciati. It is possible, therefore, that some of the original dung thrown by Rinaldeschi survives under the gilding on the rosette, which is still visible on the fresco [Figure 27], though more so in a photograph taken in the 1920s, before its restoration [Figure 26].[69]

----

[65] Ibid., examination of Giovan Battista de' Mini (10 October 1545), "Interrogatus dixit se nescire an Philippus de Dolciatis pinxerit imaginem Virginis Marie . . . et quod veritas est quod de anno 1501 dicitur dictam imaginem Virginis Marie demonstrasse miraculum quod fuit notorium et quod veritas est quod dictum oratorium novum non fuit fabricatum per annos quatuor vel circa post dictum miraculum. . . ."

[66] Ibid., examination of Geri di Poldo de' Pazzi (10 October 1545), ". . . quod nescit quisnam pinxerit dictam imaginam Virginis Marie sed seu miraculum quod asseritur factum per dictam imaginem fuit factum de anno 1501, vel circa, . . . hec scit." [. . . that he did not know who painted said image of the Virgin Mary, but asked whether the miracle that is claimed was done by said image was done in the year 1501 or thereabout, this he knew.]

[67] Ibid., examination of Niccolò di Baldo (1 July 1545), ". . . et recordatur quando dicta ecclesia fuit decorata propter miraculum quod apparuit anno 1501 vel circa propter quoddam [. . .] de Rinaldeschis fuit suspensus propter sua demerita." The blank space indicates that the speaker did not know Rinaldeschi's Christian name.

[68] See Appendix, Document II.

A second but more likely possibility is that the Virgin in some way identified Rinaldeschi as the culprit, since the *opera* register specified "how it pleased Her to uncover the matter" (in the version published by Richa, "God" appears in place of "Her"), and since the San Miniato codex attributes Rinaldeschi's discovery to a miracle of the Virgin.

Thirdly, the miracle may relate to the knife with which Rinaldeschi tried to kill himself when he was arrested and which struck a rib and did not penetrate his body, according to the record, "because it was pleasing to this merciful Virgin, who did not wish that this soul should be lost by such a misdeed." This last conjecture derives some support from the Stibbert picture, where in the scene depicting Rinaldeschi's arrest two angels are shown driving away the devils who previously instigated Rinaldeschi but who appear in no subsequent scenes except the final one, where they lose the struggle for his soul. On the contrary, Rinaldeschi is shown accompanied by an angel when he is taken from prison to his trial and after absolution to his execution, and in the final scene two angels beat off the devils and carry off Rinaldeschi's soul.[70]

It may be a mistake to search too hard for a single identifiable miracle. In spite of the reference by Niccolò di Baldo to a *miraculum* which occurred in or about 1501, in the singular, most of the sources mention signs and miracles in the plural, and it may have been precisely the plurality of miraculous phenomena that impressed contemporaries. It is hard to judge from the sources whether the cult that developed

---

[69] See the first edition [n.d. but 1926] of Torricelli, *La chiesa* (above, ch. 1 n. 4), frontispiece and 12. In the copy of this earlier edition now in the Kunsthistorisches Institut in Florence there appears below the frontispiece the written comment, perhaps in the hand of Ulrich Middeldorf, "ganzlich übermalt" ("totally overpainted"). The illustration does not appear in the 1980 edition of Torricelli (above, ch. 1 n. 4).

[70] The San Miniato codex, as published by Rondini, "I giustiziati" (above, ch. 1 n. 3), 226, said of Rinaldeschi that "per intercessione della SS. Vergine fu visto disputare l'anima sua da demoni e dagli Angeli, quali la portarono in Paradiso" [through the intercession of the most holy Virgin his soul was seen to be contested by demons and the angels who brought it to Heaven], but since a vision of the contest for his soul was not mentioned in the other records of the Company of the Blacks, nor in any of the other written sources, the statement probably reflects a later reading of the picture's final scene. On the struggles between angels and devils for the souls of dying people see A. Gurevich, *Historical Anthropology of the Middle Ages*, ed. J. Howlett (Cambridge, 1992), 97, who contrasted this "lesser" eschatology of immediate judgement with the "great" eschatology of the Last Judgment.

around the image was the result of a popular movement or of a clerical initiative, and to distinguish the roles of the ecclesiastical authorities, the secular government, and the local clergy, who doubtless participated in and encouraged the devotion. The fact that the archbishop's vicar ordered the image to be cleaned on the day of the execution suggests that some of the ecclesiastical authorities may have tried not only to remove a signal sign of dishonour to the Virgin but also to prevent the development of a cult.[71] If this was the case, however, it was apparently too late, since only four days later, on 26 July, enough gifts were coming in for the rector and members of the parish to form an *opera* to foster devotion to the image. Clearly, therefore, the clergy acted to control and take advantage of a movement that they could not easily prevent.

The devotion shown to the Madonna de' Ricci is probably to be associated with the most important of all Florentine cults concerning an image, namely the worship of the thirteenth-century painting of the Virgin preserved in the church of the Santissima Annunziata, which had been praised by Savonarola [Figure 28].[72] The painting was surrounded by so many *ex voto* figures in wax of grateful persons that it proved necessary, in 1401, to limit access to it, in this case by allowing only the *ex votos* of citizens who were entitled to hold the highest positions in the republic.[73] The prevailing sensitivity about images in the city helps to explain not only the severity with which Rinaldeschi was punished but also the unusual attention and finally the religious devotions that surrounded an episode that otherwise appears somewhat banal, if not sordid. For the parishioners of S. Maria degli Alberighi, and also for the

---

71 See Cohen, "Honor" (above, ch. 2 n. 29), on the need in cases of house-scorning to clear away marks of dishonour rapidly.

72 E. Casalini, "La Santissima Annunziata nella storia e nella civiltà fiorentina," in *Tesori d'arte dell'Annunziata di Firenze* (Florence, 1987), 75–99. We are grateful to P.H. Jolly for allowing us to read in typescript her unpublished article, "Jan Eyck's Italian Pilgrimage: A Miraculous Florentine *Annunciation* and the Ghent Altarpiece." The Annunziata was praised by Savonarola in *Prediche sopra l'Esodo*, ed. P. G. Ricci, 2 vols. (Rome, 1955–1956), I, 52 (18 February 1498).

73 Trexler, *Public Life* (above, ch. 1 n. 14), 98–99. The law of 1401 is mentioned in A. Warburg, "Bildniskunst und florentinisches Bürgertum"(1902), repr. in his *Gesammelte Schriften*, 2 vols. (Leipzig-Berlin, 1932), I, 116 n. 4, trans. in idem, *The Renewal of Pagan Antiquity*, trans D. Britt (Los Angeles, 1999), 204; see 204–208 on wax votive images at the SS. Annunziata.

other common folk of Florence, the "miracle" at the "canto de' Ricci," as the street corner was known, was in essence a moment of unveiling. The Virgin of the Annunziata, ordinarily off-limits in the Church of the Annunziata, now became visible and made her presence felt among them through the street-corner Madonna de' Ricci.

The prevailing sensitivity about images, to which Savonarola in part contributed, helps to explain not only the severity with which Rinaldeschi was punished but also the unusual attention and finally the religious devotions that surrounded the episode. His blasphemous act drew attention, in ways that varied from person to person, to an existing image of the Virgin, which immediately became the focus of popular interest and veneration. This in turn generated the signs and miracles to which the sources refer. The authorities, however, brought it under ecclesiastical control by enclosing the space and appointing guardians who restricted access and collected the offerings brought by the faithful. Seen from this point of view, the execution of Rinaldeschi was less a punishment for a specific crime than an endorsement of a development for which he had provided the catalyst. In apprehending and executing Rinaldeschi, and in supporting the building of the oratory, the Eight for Security put their powers of summary justice at the service not only of the popular regime but also of the people themselves. The magistracy was winning new legitimacy as it regularized its extraordinary powers.[74] The popular devotion and miracles that appeared during the ten days between Rinaldeschi's offence and his trial may to this extent have been decisive in determining his execution. To have spared him at that point would have put into question both the honour and the power of the Virgin and the legitimacy of the devotion to her image.

---

[74]Zorzi argues in the conclusion to his article on "Esecuzioni" (above, ch. 1 n. 3), 58–60, that the transformation and systematization of the ceremonies of execution were important aspects of the emergence and affirmation of state power in Florence and that as "l'archetipo della purificazione rituale" [the archetype of ritual purification] it renewed the promise of order and stability on which the new authority was based. Compare also Machiavelli, *Discourses* (n. 12 above), I, 12, 95, where, commenting on a miraculous statue of Juno reported in Livy (5.22), he writes that prudent statesmen will "augment" religious miracles in order to earn faith or credit. Although Machiavelli does not mention the Rinaldeschi episode in his writings, he was in Florence during these events. He left on a mission to Pistoia on 23 July 1501, the day after Rinaldeschi's hanging.

Figure 1. Filippo Dolciati, *Rinaldeschi loses at dice*.

Inscribed (at top): "ADI 21 DI LVGLIO MDI" [On the 21st day of July, 1501]; and (at bottom): "Ant.º di Giu:ᵉ Rinaldeschi nobile fiorentino nell' Osteria del fico / Gioca e Persi i danari e i Panni accecato dall'ira . . ." [Antonio di Giuseppe Rinaldeschi, a Florentine nobleman, gambles in the tavern of the Fig-Tree, and having lost his money and his clothes, blinded by anger . . . .]

Figures 1–10 reproduced by permission of the Museo Stibbert.

Figure 2. *Rinaldeschi gathers dung.*

Inscribed: "... Raccoglie sterco di cavallo stimolato dal / diavolo . . . ."
[. . . gathers horse dung, spurred by the devil.]

Figure 3. *Rinaldeschi throws dung at the Virgin.*

Inscribed: "Getta lo sterco in faccia della / Beata Vergine Bestemmiando e fugge in Villa." [He throws the dung in the face of the Blessed Virgin, swearing, and flees to a country house.]

Figure 4. *The arrest of Rinaldeschi.*

Inscribed: "Listesso di e preso / e pentitosi / si caccia un coltello / nel petto." [The same day he is taken, and, repenting, he thrusts a knife into his breast.]

Figure 5. *Rinaldeschi taken to Florence.*

Inscribed: "Lo conducono in fiorenza." [They conduct him to Florence.]

Figure 6.   *Rinaldeschi led from his cell.*

Inscribed: "Lo cavano di prigione e lo Conducono ad / Esaminarsi." [They take him from prison and conduct him to be examined.]

Figure 7. *Examination by the Eight.*

Inscribed: "Esaminato avanti i S:S: Otto / confessa et a 24 ore di notte
/ per sentenza . . . " [After being examined by the Eight lords, he
confesses, and at the twenty-fourth hour of the night, in accordance
with the sentence . . .]

Figure 8. *Rinaldeschi's confession.*

Inscribed: "... dal carnefice e condotto alla Morte." [... he is conducted to his death by the executioner.]

Figure 9. *The hanging of Rinaldeschi.*

Inscribed (at left): "SIGNIOR·MIO / GIESV.CHRIS / TOABI MISE / RICHORDIA / DELANIMA / MIA·" [My Lord, Jesus Christ, have mercy on my soul]; and (at bottom): "A VII Ore di notte è impiccato a le finestre del / Potestà e in sepoltura il dì di S. Maria Maddalena." [At the seventh hour of the night he is hanged from the windows of the Podestà and he is buried on the day of Saint Mary Magdalene.]

Figure 10. Filippo Dolciati, *The History of Antonio Rinaldeschi*.
Florence, Museo Stibbert. Painted in 1502. Overall view.

83

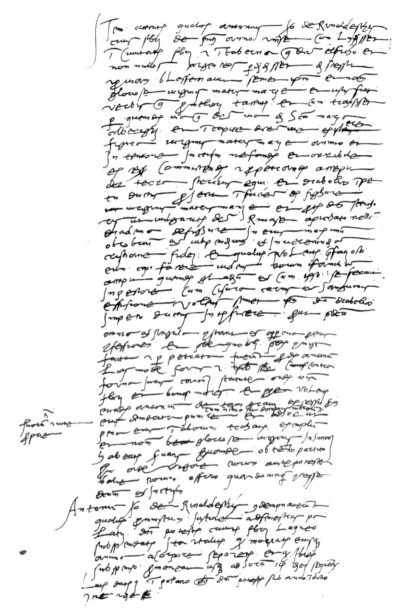

Figure 11. The sentence of the Eight for Security against
Antonio Rinaldeschi.

Archivio di Stato, Florence, Otto di guardia e balìa, Periodo
repubblicano, 120, fol. 128^{r-v}. By permission of the Ministero
per i Beni e le Attività Culturali.

84

Figure 12. *Image of Infamy on the Palace of the Podestà*, engraving by Vincenzo Cavini after a drawing by Giuseppe Manni.

From Angelo Poliziano, *Conjurationis Pactianae anni MCCCCLXXVIII commentarium*, ed. G. Adimari (Naples, 1769), 139. British Library shelf mark 1197.f.13. By permission of the British Library.

Figure 13. Filippino Lippi, *St. Paul Visiting St. Peter in Prison.*

Florence, Church of S. Maria del Carmine, Brancacci Chapel.

86

Figure 14. Duccio di Buoninsegna, *Christ Taken Prisoner*.
Siena, Museo dell'Opera del Duomo. Archivio Fotografico Electra.

Gallows   "The Temple"

Figure 15. Gallows and the chapel known as "The Temple." Detail from *Mappa della Catena*, circa 1470.

Florence, Museo di Firenze com'era. Photo: Scala / Art Resource NY.

88

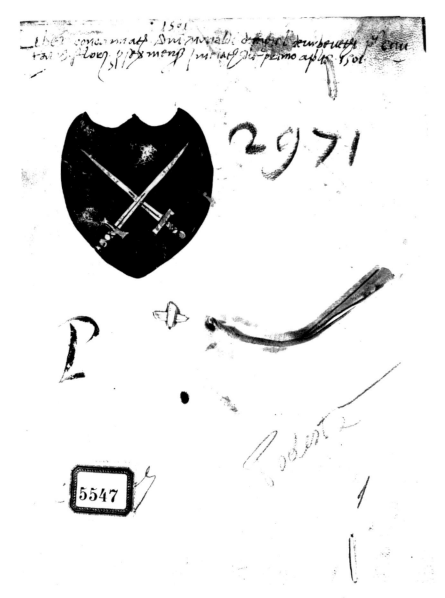

Figure 16. Cover of the "Liber condemnationum" of Messer Monaldo de' Fascioli of Orvieto, Podestà of Florence in 1501, with his coat-of-arms.

Archivio di Stato, Florence, Atti del Podestà, 5547. By permission of the Ministero per i Beni e le Attività Culturali.

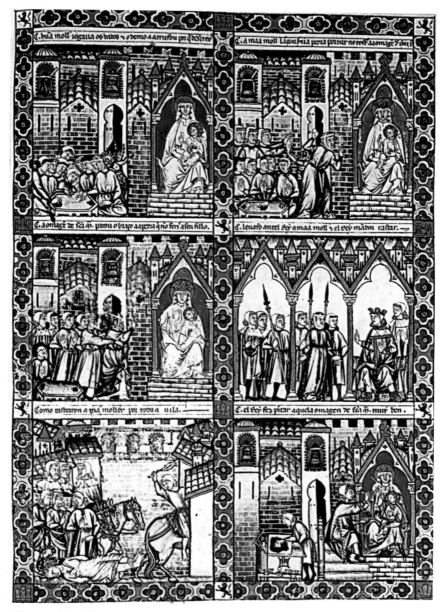

Figure 17. Illustration of Cantiga 136 from the Escorial Codex of the *Cantigas de Santa Maria* of Alfonso the Wise.

Biblioteca de San Lorenzo el Real de El Escorial, codex T.I.1, fol. 192[r]. By permission of the Patrimonio Nacional.

Figure 18. Illustration of Cantiga 294 from the Florence Codex of the *Cantigas de Santa Maria* of Alfonso the Wise.

Biblioteca Nazionale Centrale, Florence, Banco Rari, 20, fol. 20^r.
By permission of the Ministero per i Beni e le Attività Culturali.

Figure 19. Illustration of Cantiga 154 from the Escorial Codex of the *Cantigas de Santa Maria* of Alfonso the Wise.

Biblioteca de San Lorenzo el Real de El Escorial, codex T.I.1, fol. 209ʳ. By permission of the Patrimonio Nacional.

Figure 20. Fra Bartolomeo. *Portrait of Girolamo Savonarola.*

Florence, Museo di S. Marco.
Photo: Scala / Art Resource NY.

Figure 21. Anonymous artist, *Execution of Savonarola and Two Followers in the Piazza of the Signoria, 23 May 1498.*

Florence, Museo di S. Marco.
Photo: Erich Lessing / Art Resource NY.

94

Figure 22   View of S. Maria degli Alberighi, circa 1447.

Florence, Biblioteca del Seminario Arcivescovile Maggiore di Cestello, codex of Marco di Bartolommeo Rustici.

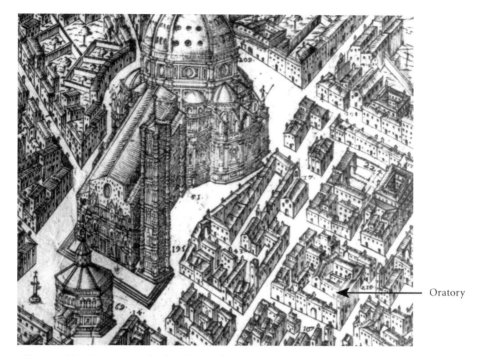

Oratory

Figure 23. S. Maria degli Alberighi and the oratory constructed by Baccio d'Agnolo.

Detail from the map of Florence by Stefano Buonsignori, *Nova Pulcherrimae civitatis Florentiae topographia accuratissime delineata* (Florence 1584). Photo: Kunsthistorisches Institut, Max-Planck-Institut, Florence.

96

Figure 24. Florence, Church of the Madonna de' Ricci, façade on the Via del Corso.

Archivio Fotografico Alinari.

Figure 25. *Madonna de' Ricci*, detail of Figure 3.

Figure 26. *Madonna de' Ricci*, fresco. Florence, Church of the Madonna de' Ricci, before restoration.

From C. Torricelli, *La Chiesa della Madonna de' Ricci* (Florence, [1926]).

Figure 27. *Madonna de' Ricci*, fresco. Florence, Church of the Madonna de' Ricci.

Photograph taken in 1995.

Figure 28. *Annunziata*, panel painting. Florence, Church of the SS. Annunziata.

Archivio Fotografico Alinari.

Appendix of Documents

Document I.

The sentence of the Eight for Security against Antonio Rinaldeschi.

[ASF, OGB, 120, fol. 128^{r-v} (21 July 1501) with photograph in Figure 11].

Item attendentes qualiter Antonius Iohannis de Rinaldeschis, civis Florentinus, de presenti anno et mense, cum ludisset in civitate Florentie, et in taberna qua dicitur "El Ficho," et non nullos argenteos perdidisset, discessit, et per viam blasfemavit semet ipsum et nominem gloriose virginis matris Marie, et usus fuit verbis quae pro meliori tacentur, et cum transisset per quemdam viam quae dicitur "via di Sancta Maria Alberighi," et in capite dicte vie existeret[1] figura virginis matris Marie, animo et intentione in ceterum nefandum et orribile excessum commictendi et perpetrandi, accepit de terra sterchum equi, et diabolico impetu ductus, proiecit in faciem dicte fighure virginis[2] matris Marie, et parte dicti[3] sterchoris, ut vulghariter dicitur, "rimase apichato nella diadema" dicte fighure, in eius maximum obrobrium ac vilipendium, et in verecundiam cristiane fidei. Et qualiter volentes prefati Octo eum capi facere, videns eorum familiam, accepit quemdam gladium, et cum ipso se ferivit in pectore, cum cisura carnis et sanguinis effusione, volens semet ipsum, dicto diabolico impetu ductus, interficere, prout predicta [128^v] omnia et singula constant et apparent per eius confessionem, et predicta et quodlibet predictorum, commissa, facta et perpetrata fuerunt per dictum Antonium, locis, modis, formis, et temporibus suprascriptis, contra[4] formam iuris canonici, statutorum, ordinamentorum Comunis Florentie, et bonos mores. Et propterea volentes, eundem Antonium de tam gravi excessu, secundum eius demerita, punire, cum nemo sit dominus membrorum suorum, et vite proprie, et ad hoc ut pena eius in

---

[1] ms: "existens" changed to "existeret"
[2] cancelled: "ut"
[3] ms: "dictus"
[4] cancelled: "cons[uetudines?] . . ."

aliorum trahatur exemplum, et nomen beate gloriose verginis in honorem habeatur, servatis servandis, obtento partito secundum ordinamento, vigore eorum auctoritatis, potestatis, balie eorum officio quandocunque concesse, dictum et infrascriptum

Antonium Iohannis de Rinaldeschis condemnaverunt qualiter per ministrum iustitie ad fenestras palatii domini Potestatis civitatis Florentie laqueo subspendatur ita et taliter quod moriatur, eiusque anima a corpore separetur. Et quod ibidem subspensus[5] permaneat usque ad horam 14 diei sequentis.

Latum, datum, etc. in palatio dicti domini Potestatis sub anno indictione et die suprascriptis.

★   ★   ★

Item. Considering whereas Antonius Iohannis de Rinaldeschis, a Florentine citizen, in the present year and month, after he had gambled in the city of Florence, in a tavern that is called "The Fig Tree," and had lost much silver coin, went out and along the way blasphemed himself and the name of the glorious virgin mother Mary, and used words that are better kept silent, and when he had gone through a certain street which is called "Via di Santa Maria Alberighi," and at the head of said street there was a figure of the virgin mother Mary, with the spirit and intention of committing and perpetrating another unspeakable and horrible crime, he gathered horse dung from the ground, and, guided by a diabolical force, he threw it at the face of said figure of the virgin mother Mary, and part of said dung, as is said in the vernacular, "remained stuck in the diadem" of said figure, to her great dishonour and disgrace and to the shame of the Christian faith, and whereas, when the said Eight wished to have him arrested, when he saw their patrol, he grasped a certain dagger, and with it he wounded himself in the breast, with the cutting of flesh and the spilling of blood, since he wished, guided by said diabolical force, to kill himself, just as all and each of the aforesaid things stand and appear in his own confession, and the aforesaid and any of the aforesaid things, were committed, done and perpetrated by said Antonius, in the places, ways, forms and times written above, against the form of canon law, of the statutes and ordinances of the Commune of Florence, and good behaviour. Wishing therefore to punish the said Antonius for such a serious crime according

---

5 ms: "subspenso"

to his offences, since no one should be lord of his limbs and of his own life, and in order that his punishment might be an example for others, and that the name of the blessed, glorious Virgin may be held in honour, having observed what should be observed, and having taken a vote in accordance with the law, by vigour of their authority, of their power, and of the extraordinary force of their office whensoever this was conferred, they condemned the said and below named Antonius Iohannis de Rinaldeschis, so that by the minister of justice he should be hanged with a rope from the windows of the palace of the lord Podestà of the city of Florence in such a way and to such a degree that he dies and his soul is separated from his body. And he should remain hanged in the same place until the fourteenth hour of the following day.

Delivered, issued, etc. in the palace of said lord Podestà in the year and indiction and on the day written above.

Document II.

"Narration of the Crime of Rinaldesco," from the account book of the *opera* of the Madonna de' Ricci, in the hand of Giovanni Landi.
[Banc., MSS, 54, "Entrata, uscita, debitori, creditori, e ricordanze", fol. 131^r].

+ yhs. Maria. MD1°.//.

Ricordo chome insino a' dì 11 di luglio 1501, passando Antonio Rinaldeschi per la piazuola di Santa Maria Alberighi, richolse di terra una manata[1] di stercho di chavallo overo d'asino, e quando e' fu pasato la detta piazzuola e g[i]unto nel chiasolino che va nella via di Porzanpiero, si voltò alla fighura della Nostra Donna Nunziata che è dipinta sopra la porta di fiancho di detta chiesa, e gittogli quello stercho, el quale era alido, mediante l'essere stato per aventura qualche dì al sole, e miracholosamente gliene rimase un pocho apichata nella diadema sopra la cholottola, tanta che quasi pareva una rosetta secha. E anchora che 'l detto Antonio non fussi da persona veduto gittare simile sporcizia nella detta Nunziata, e chome piacque a lei la chosa si schoperir, e' venne a notizia a l'ufic[i]o degli Otto, e quali chonmetter bandi, sotto grave pene, chi sapessi el detto Antonio e no' llo insengniassi, in modo ch' egl' ebono notizia che s'era fugito fuori di Firenze e in che luogho di che mandorono la loro famiglia a pigliarllo; di che, chome el detto Antonio si vide soprag[i]unto dalla detta famiglia da sse medesimo si dette di uno choltello nel petto. Et chome piacque a essa miserichordiosa Vergine, che non volle però che per tanto eccesso che quella anima si perdessi, el detto choltello trovò una chostola, in modo che non passò drento, di che e' fu menatone preso a' dì 21 di detto mese. E inmediate fu disaminato da' detti Signori Otto, e quali lo trovorono cholpevole, e lui medesimo si g[i]udichò esser dengnio della morte per tanto eccesso quanto egli aveva fatto; di che e' lo sentenziorono alla morte, e detto dì fu inpichato, circha a ore. . . .[2] alle finestre del Chapitano, e lasciato stare morto, e chosì inpichato insino alla mattina vengniente che fu a' dì 22 di detto. E detta mattina messer Lodovico Adimari, vichario

---

[1] ms: "menata"
[2] blank in ms.

dello arcivescovo di Firenze, mandò. . . . ,[3] prete, a spichare el detto stercho dalla detta Nostra Donna.

[Note at bottom, in a seventeenth-century hand:]
Primo richordo quando gittò Antonio Rinaldeschi la brutura alla nostra Nunziata.

★   ★   ★

+ Jesus. Mary. 1501.

Record. How on the 11th day of July, 1501, as Antonio Rinaldeschi was passing through the little piazza of Santa Maria Alberighi, he gathered from the ground a handful of dung from a horse, or rather an ass, and when he had left said little piazza and reached the small alley that goes into the Via di Porta San Piero, he turned to the figure of Our Lady Annunciate, which is painted above the side-door of said church, and he threw that dung, which was dry, since it had been by chance some days in the sun, and miraculously a bit of it remained stuck in the diadem above the nape of her neck, so that it almost resembled a dry rosette. And although said Antonio was not seen by anyone throwing such filth at said [Virgin] Annunciate, because it pleased her that the thing be revealed, it came to the attention of the office of the Eight, who imposed heavy penalties on whoever knew said Antonio and did not tell them, with the result that they had notice that he had fled outside Florence, and in what place, whereupon they sent their patrol to arrest him. Whereupon, when said Antonio saw that he was overtaken by said patrol, he thrust a knife into his chest. And, because it was pleasing to this merciful Virgin, who did not wish that this soul should be lost by such a misdeed, said knife found a rib, so that it did not enter him, whereupon he was arrested and led away on the 21st day of said month. And immediately he was examined by the said Eight Lords, who found him guilty, and he himself judged he merited death for a crime so great as the one he had committed. Whereupon they sentenced him to death, and on said day he was hanged, at about . . . hours, from the windows of the Palace of the Captain.[4] And he was left to stay there dead and hanged thus until the next morning, which was on the 22nd day of said month. And on said morning messer Lodovico Adimari, the vicar of the

---

3 blank in ms.
4 "Palace of the Captain": the Palace of the Podestà was also known as the Palace of the Captain or of the Bargello.

archbishop of Florence, sent. . . . , a priest, to clean said dung from said Our Lady.

The first record of when Antonio Rinaldeschi threw the filth at our Annunciate.

Document III.

A notice from records kept by the Company of the Blacks.

[BNCF, Fondo nazionale, II.I.138, fols. 67^r-144^r, "Notizzie . . . cavate da un libro della venerabile Compagnia di S. Maria della Croce al Tempio," fol. 81^r. See also above, ch. 1 n. 4.]

Antonio di Giovanni Rinaldeschi. Inpiccato alle finestre del Potestà all'ore 2 di notte, 22 luglio. E quinci stette insino all'altro dì, che ci è la festa di S. Maria Maddalena. Perché per disperazione inbrattò con sterco la figura di Nostra Donna agl'Alberighi. Et in detto dì, in quel luogo, la devozione e[1] concorso delle persone cominciò e segue.

$\star$ $\star$ $\star$

Antonio di Giovanni Rinaldeschi. Hanged from the windows of the Podestà at the second hour of the night, the 22nd of July. And he remained there until the next day, which is the Feast of St. Mary Magdalene. For in despair he befouled with dung the figure of Our Lady at the Alberighi. And on said day, in that place, the devotion and thronging of persons began and ensues.

---

[1] cancelled: "preg[hiere?] . . ."

Document IV.

A second notice from records kept by the Company of the Blacks.

[Copied in 1637 by Bernardo Giuliani, in APTPS, Reg. Dom., 505, S.M.R., 15, "Documenti relativi a S. Maria de' Ricci dalle origini," fol. 4^{r-v}].

In un libro di Memorie della Compagnia[1] di Sta Maria della Croce a Tempio, detta la Compagnia grande del Tempio, appresso di me, Bernardo di messer Lelio di ser Bernardo Giuliani, Cancelliere di detta Compagnia, quale è coperto di cartapecora biancha, antico e consumato, di carta bambagina in quarto, nel quale vi è molte memorie di iustiziati nel 1356 alli 28 d'aprile e via[2] seguendo, sì che a carte 61 vi si vede quanto appresso:

1501. 430—Antonio di Giovanni Rinaldeschi fu imo peso alle finestre del podestà a' dì 21 di luglio la sera, a ore una di notte. Fu preso il medesimo dì. Ebbe dua ore di tempo. Costui era gran bestemmiatore, battitore di Padre, e haveva bruttato la nostra Donna di Santa Maria Alberighi. Dettesi di un coltello nella poppa manca quando si vedde la famiglia addosso. Giudicossi al Tempio. Per non essere dal popolo [4^v] strascinato, chiedeva di gratia di essere impiccato ivi. Fugli fatta, e fu sotterrato al Tempio.

Bernardo Giuliani, Cancelliere, questo dì 13 di Maggio 1637.

★   ★   ★

In a book of records of the Company of S. Maria della Croce al Tempio, called the Great Company of the Temple, which is with me, Bernardo di Messer Lelio di Bernardo Giuliani, chancellor of said company, which is covered in parchment, old and consumed, of cotton paper in quarto, in which there are many records of persons executed, beginning in 1356, from the 28th of April, and following from then, such that on page 61[3] one sees there the following:

---

[1] cancelled: "del"

[2] ms: "va"

[3] Commonly only the right page of an opened book was numbered. In sixteenth-century usage the Italian *carte* (literally "pages" in the plural) refers to both the left and right pages visible at a given page number.

1501. [Number] 430.[4] Antonio di Giovanni Rinaldeschi was disgrace-
fully hanged from the windows of the Podestà on the 21st of July in the
evening, at the hour of one at night. He was taken the same day. He
had two hours to live. He was a great blasphemer, a beater of his father,
and he had befouled Our Lady of Santa Maria Alberighi. He thrust a
knife into his left breast when he saw the patrol was upon him. He was
judged in the Temple. So as not to be torn to pieces by the people, he
requested the favour of being hanged there. He received this favour and
he was buried at the Temple.

Bernardo Giuliani, chancellor, this the 13th day of May, 1637.

---

[4] Rinaldeschi's execution must have been 430th in the list from which this was
copied.

Document V.

From the *Diary* of Luca Landucci.

[Published in Luca Landucci, *Diario fiorentino dal 1450 al 1516*, ed. I. del Badia (Florence, 1883), 233–234].

E a dì 21 di luglio 1501, fu preso uno che à nome Rinaldo, fiorentino, ch'era giucatore; el quale, perchè aveva perduto, gittò sterco di cavallo a una Vergine Maria ch'è dal Canto de' Ricci in uno chiassolino da quella Chiesa ch'è in su una piazzuola di dietro alle case; e dettegli nella diadema. E vedendolo un fanciullo disse come egli era stato un uomo; e fugli andato dietro e codiato, e fu preso all'Osservanza di San Miniato, e quando e famigli degli Otto gli furono presso si dette d'un coltellino nella poppa manca, e loro lo presono e menoronlo al Podestà, e confessò averlo gittato per passione d'avere perduto, e la notte lo impiccorono alle finestre del Podestà, e fu la mattina di Santa Maria Maddalena, che fu una festa doppia. Vi venne tutto Firenze a vedere, per modo che venendo el Vescovo a vedere questa Vergine Maria, levò detto sterco da lei, in modo che non fu sera che vi fu appiccato molte libbre di cera, e tutta volta crescendo la divozione. E in pochi dì vi venne tante immagini come si vedrà col tempo.

★   ★   ★

And on the 21st of July 1501 there was arrested a man of the name Rinaldo, a Florentine, who was a gambler. This man, because he had lost, threw horse dung at a Virgin Mary which is at the Canto de' Ricci in a small alley by that church which is in the little piazza behind the houses, and he struck it in the diadem. And a child saw him who said that he was a grown man, and he was pursued and tailed, and he was taken at the Observancy of San Miniato, and when the patrol of the Eight were close to him he struck himself with a small knife in the left breast, and they took him and led him to the Podestà, and he confessed that he had thrown it out of passion at having lost, and at night they hanged him from the windows of the Podestà, and the next morning was the feast of Saint Mary Magdalene, which was a double-feast. All Florence came to see, so that when the Bishop came to see this Virgin Mary he cleaned her of said dung, so that, before evening came, many pounds of wax were hung there as all the while the devotion grew. And in a few days a great many images were brought there as shall be seen afterward.

Document VI.

From a seventeenth-century miscellany compiled by Carlo Strozzi.

[Carlo Strozzi, "Raccolta di memorie, fondazioni, e padronati di diverse chiese, monasteri, spedali, compagnie e simili fatta dal senatore Carlo di Tommaso Strozzi," ms in ASF, CS, ser. III, 233, fol. 130ᵛ].

Madonna de' Ricci o Nunziata de' Ricci.
La devozione della Madonna, che si chiama de' [Ricci][1] per essere quivi intorno le case di quella famiglia, hebbe principio da questo caso l'anno 1501. Un Rinaldo. . . .[2], giocatore, haveva perso buona somma di danaro, e, passando da quel luogo, dove allhora era una stradella in sul canto della quale era un inmagine della Madonna, gettò sterco di cavallo alla detta inmagine, e colpilla nella diadema. Et essendo da un fanciullo stato visto, fu codiato e corsoli dreto e raggiunto all'Osservanza di San Miniato. Et egli, quando si vedde i[3] famigli degl' Otto vicini, si dette con un coltello nella poppa manca. E, fatto prigione, fu condotto al Palazzo del Podestà. E confessò haverlo fatto per passione, e la notte stessa fu impiccato alle finestre del detto Palazzo, e fu la mattina di Santa Maria Maddalena. Corse gran gente a vedere quella santa inmagine; e dal Vescovo fu levata quella bruttura; e non fu sera che quivi furono appese molte libbre di cera, et in pochi giorni gran quantità di voti. E, continuando la devozione, l' anno 1508 fu fondata la chiesa dove di presente si trova la detta devota inmagine, nella quale chiesa Madonna Lucrezia Salviati Medici, l'anno 1530, fondò due cappelle.

★   ★   ★

Madonna de' Ricci or Nunziata of the Ricci.
The devotion of the Madonna who is called "of the Ricci" because the houses of that family are all around her had its beginning in the following occurrence in the year 1501. A Rinaldo. . . . a gambler, had lost a good sum of money, and, while passing that place, where then there was a small street, on the corner of which there was an image of the Madonna, threw horse dung at said image, and struck her in her diadem. And since

---

[1] missing in ms.
[2] blank in ms.
[3] cancelled: "birri vicini"

he was seen by a boy, he was followed and run after and overtaken at the Observancy of San Miniato. And he, when he saw that the patrol of the Eight was near, stabbed himself with a knife in the left breast. Once he was made prisoner he was taken to the Palace of the Podestà. He confessed that he had done it out of passion, and that same night he was hanged from the windows of said palace, and in the morning it was the feast of Saint Mary Magdalene. A great crowd ran to see that holy image, and the filth was removed by the bishop, and before evening many pounds of wax were hung there, and in a few days a great many ex votos. As the devotion continued, in the year 1508 the church where at present said devotional image is found was established, in which church in the year 1530 Madonna Lucrezia Salviati Medici established two chapels.

Document VII.

A record copied from a *priorista* that belonged to Matteo Segaloni in 1630.

[APTPS, Reg. Dom., 505, S.M.R. 15, "Documenti relativi a S. Maria de' Ricci dalle origini," fol. 5^{r-v}].

Da uno Priorista, existente oggi, questo dì 10 di giugno 1630, nella casa et appresso il signore Matteo Segaloni.

+ A' dì 21 di luglio 1501.

Fu uno che si chiamava il Rinaldescho, havendo giucato e perduto, come huomo bestiale andò alla Vergine Maria, hoggi chiamata delli Alberighi[1], e gettolli nel viso una manata di stercho di cavallo. E rimasele appiccato nell'volto, e per permessione de Dio, fu veduto, e gli Otto lo seppono. E saputo lui che gli Otto l'havevano presentito, si fugge in villa sua, e lassu fu trovato da' famigli. E lui medesimo, ch[e][2] non poteva fuggire da loro, perché era attengiato e doglioso di mal francioso, si dette di uno coltello per ammazzarsi. Ma Iddio non volle, perché menato fu a Firenze, la notte medesima si confessò, et avvidesi haver fatto grande errore, e da sse si giudicò la morte, ma pregò che non fussi dato al popolo, perché era gran popolo per vederlo fuori. Fu impiccato, et stette tutto il dì impiccato di Santa Maria Maddalena, sì che tutto Firenze lo vedde. E per dimostrare la sua potenza, Iddio, [5^{v}] in favore di quella Vergine del Cielo sua Madre, cominciò a fare di molti miracoli, di modo si cominciò a edificare e disfare assai botteghe per farvi una bella chiesa, che a Dio piaccia dare animo a chi può d'aiutare si seguiti, et insino al fine, di finire la chiesa come hanno cominciato.

★   ★   ★

From a *priorista* that exists today, this the 10th day of June, 1630, in the house and in the possession of signore Matteo Segaloni.

+ On the 21st day of July, 1501.

There was a man called "Il Rinaldescho," who having gambled and lost, like a bestial man went to the Virgin Mary, today called "of the

---

[1] ms: "Aberighi"
[2] ms damaged

Alberighi", and threw in her face a handful of horse dung. And it remained stuck on her face, and with God's permission he was seen and the Eight learned of it. And when he found out that the Eight suspected him he fled to his country house and up there he was found by the patrol. And he himself, since he could not flee from them, because he was infected and in pain from the French disease, stabbed himself with a knife in order to kill himself. But God did not wish it, so that he was led to Florence, that same night he confessed, and he recognized that he had committed a great error, and he judged himself as meriting death, but he begged that he not be given to the people, because outside there was a great crowd of people watching for him. He was hanged, and he remained hanging the whole day of Saint Mary Magdalene, so that all Florence saw him. And to show his power, God, as a show of favour toward that Virgin in Heaven his Mother, began to work many miracles, so that to build a beautiful church the construction and the demolition of many shops began, may it please God to give spirit to whoever can help so that it continues to the end and the church that has been begun may be finished.

Document VIII

Payments to the painter Filippo Dolciati in the account book of the *opera* of the Madonna de' Ricci, in the hand of Giovanni Landi.
[1 payment recorded in Banc., MSS, 54, fol. 21^r (24 February 1501/2)].

Muraglia, lire dodici di piccioli per lei a Filippo Dolc[i]ati dipintore, avere al mio quaderno di cassa segnato "A," a carte 6, per dipintura e cholori del sopracielo della chapella della Nunziata, e mettere le stella, e chosì dove si racconciò l'usc[i]o in detta chapella fornire la spalliera in detta chapella, e per dipingnere 3 Profeti. Al libro, a carte 9:

f.-, l. 12,-

[2 payments recorded *ibid.*, fol. 22^r (24 March 1501/2)].

Muraglia, lire sette di piccioli per loro a Filippo di Lorenzo Dolc[i]ati dipintore, avere al quaderno di chassa segnato "A," a carte 9. Sono per dipintura di una Piatà dipinse nella facc[i]a dinanzi della altare della Nunziata e per dipintura della predella per in su l'altare e de' pilastri e bechategli e per mettere d'oro a detta predella e bechategli e per dipingnere d'azuro sopra l'altare e mettere di stella d'achordo. Al libro, a carte 15:

f.-, l. 7,-

Muraglia, lire sette, soldi 7, di piccioli per loro a Filippo di Lorenzo Dolc[i]ati e per lui a maestro Andrea barbiere, avere al quaderno di chassa segnato "A," a carte 9. Sono per tanti spese in 166 pezzi d'oro per dorare la sopradetta predella dello altare e cholonette e bechategli, e per azurro e gesso e cholla e chalcina, e a 1° scharpelino, e per mettere la p[. . . za?] dell'opera benedetta dirimpetto a l'altare, e altro d'achordo. Al libro, a carte 15:

f.-, l.7, s.7,-

★   ★   ★

[1 payment recorded on 24 February 1501/2].

Building.[1] Twelve lire common coinage from the *opera* to Filippo

---

[1] Evidently these payments were copied and cross-referenced to a set of "Building" accounts once kept in the same account book in a section (fols. 7r-20v) that is now missing.

Dolciati, painter, recorded as paid in my cashbox notebook labeled "A," on page 6, for painting and colours for the ceiling of the chapel of the Annunciate, and for putting in stars, and for similarly adjusting the paneling in said chapel where the door in said chapel was fixed, and for painting 3 prophets. In this book, on page 9:

f.-, l.12, -

[2 payments recorded on 24 March 1501/2].

Building. Seven lire common coinage from them [the *operai*] to Filippo di Lorenzo Dolciati, painter, recorded as paid in the cashbox notebook labeled "A," on page 9. This is for painting a Pietà on the face of the altar of the Annunciate, and for painting the predella to go up on the altar, and the pilasters and the capitals, and for putting the gold on said predella and capitals, and for painting with blue above the altar, and putting stars there as agreed. In this book, on page 15:

f.-, l. 7, -

Building. Seven lire, soldi 7, common coinage, from them [the *operai*] to Filippo di Lorenzo Dolciati and from him to maestro Andrea the barber, recorded as paid in the cashbox notebook labeled "A," on page 9. This is for what was spent on 166 pieces of gold to gild the above-mentioned predella of the altar and the small columns and capitals, and for azure and gesso and glue and slaked lime, and for a stoneworker, and for putting the [. . . ?] of the blessed *opera* opposite the altar and other things as agreed. In this book, on page 15:

f.-, l. 7, s. 7, -

Document IX.

The decision of the *opera* to hire the architect Baccio d'Agnolo to build a new oratory for the Madonna de' Ricci.
[ASF, NA 7981, Ser Francesco da Romena, no. 195 (2 September 1507)]

Die secunda settembris 1507.

Spettabiles viri Presbiter Batista, rector ecclesie Sancte Marie Alberighi de Florentia, et Iohannes Pieri de Landis, G[i]orgius Pieri de Riccis, Bernardus de Donatis, Bartolomeus de Pandolfinis, Ieronimus ser Pauli de Benivenis, et Franciscus Filippi del Pugl[i]ese, omnes operarii opere Sancte Marie Anunptiate predicte, in dicta ecclesia simul coadunati in eorum solita residentia, absentibus Francisco del Citadino, Ugutione de Ricis, Ieronimo de Adimaribus et Piero de Adimaribus eorum collegiis, et attendentes qualiter ad devotionem inmag[i]nis Sancte Marie Anunptiate predicte confluunt maxima mulitudo hominum et personarum tam masculum quam feminarum ad devotionem dicte inmaginis Anunptiate, et quod propterea fuit et est necessarium providere et hedificare unum oratorium sive ecclesiam, et propterea facere fecerunt modellum lignaminis pro confitiendo dictum oratorium magistro Bartolomeo Angeli legnaiuolo, in huiusmodi exercitio perito, qui dictum modellum perfecit et in dicta capella plures dies publice stetit ut si aliquid defettum in eo esset, deleretur. Et habito colloquio cum pluribus hominibus in dicto exercito peritis, qui approbaverunt dictum modellum fuisse et esse bene confettum et factum; et confidentes de prudentia et virtute ditti magistri Bartolomei, omni modo quo potuerunt, servatis servandis et obtento partito per omnes fabas nigras, deliberaverunt et ordinaverunt et eligerunt in capud magistrum ditte muraglie fiende per dictos operarios dictum magistrum Bartolomeum, reservando eisdem operariis autoritatem addendi et minuendi et mutandi omne id quod eisdem modellum videbitur esse opportunum et prout eis videbitur et placebit. [ᵛ] Et cum salario florenorum trium largorum de auro in auro quolibet mense, incipiendo ea die qua per dittos operarios incipiet facere fundamenta et dictum hedifitium faciendum cum hac conditione, quod quandocunque dictus Bartolomeus non posset presens esse ad huiusmodi exercendum et faciendum, quod ex nunc prout et ex tunc prout nunc, intelligatur elettus et institutus Antonio de Sancto Gallo pro tempore quo dictus magister Bartolomeus non posset huiusmodi exercere et pro huiusmodi salario durante tempore ditti impedimenti, et cum autoritate posse apuntare magistros et operarios venientes ad laborandum pro dicto magisterio ditti hedifitii.

Et quod floreni duo largi de auro in auro habiti per dictum magistrum Bartolomeum pro faciendo dicto modello sint pro omni eo quo posset petere usque in presentem diem, et casu quod dicti operarii firmarent dicta muramenta [non] fienda ut supra, quod ditti magistri Bartolomeus seu Antonius predicti non habeant dictum salarium dictorum trium florenorum in mense dicto tempore.
[. . .]

★   ★   ★

On the second day of September, 1507.

The honourable men, Priest Batista, rector of the church of Santa Maria Alberighi in Florence, and Iohannes Pieri de Landis, Giorgius Pieri de Riccis, Bernardus de Donatis, Bartolomeus de Pandolfinis, Ieronimus ser Pauli de Benivenis, and Franciscus Filippi del Pugliese, all of them *operai* of the *opera* of the aforesaid Saint Mary Annunciate, meeting at the same time in said church in their usual meeting place, absent their colleagues Franciscus del Citadino, Ugutio de Ricis, Ieronimus de Adimaribus and Piero de Adimaribus, considering whereas the greatest multitude of people, consisting of persons both masculine and feminine, throngs to the devotion of the image of the aforesaid Saint Mary Annunciate, and that for this reason it was and is necessary to provide and to build an oratory or church, and for this reason they had a model of wood made by master Bartolomeus Angeli, the woodworker,[1] who is skilled in this trade, to demonstrate said oratory, and he finished said model, and it stood in said chapel in public for many days so that if there were it any defect in it it could be eliminated. And having consulted many men who are skilled in said trade and who agreed that said model was and is well confected and made, and trusting in the prudence and virtue of said master Bartolomeus, in all ways that they can, having observed what needs to be observed, and having obtained a vote with all black beans,[2] they decreed and ordered and elected as the chief master

---

[1] The architect Baccio d'Agnolo is called a "woodworker" (*legnaiuolus*). "Baccio" is a shortened form of Bartolommeo.

[2] At Florence beans were typically used to count votes, black beans being affirmative and white ones negative.

of said building project for said *operai* said master Bartolomeus, reserving to the same *operai* the authority to add and subtract and change all that they think opportune in the same model, according as it seems fitting and pleases them. And with a salary of three broad gold florins for each month, beginning on the day on which he begins on behalf of said *operai* to lay foundations and to build said building, with this condition, that whensoever said Bartolomeus cannot be present to work and to build in this way, that as though from now forward, and from then as though from now, Antonius de Sancto Gallo[3] shall be understood to have been elected and confirmed for the time in which said master Bartolomeus cannot work in this way and for the same salary for the duration of said impediment, and with authority to appoint masters and workers coming to work on the project of said building.

And that the two broad gold florins received by said master Bartolomeus for making said model are all that he may request down to the present day, and, in case said *operai* decide that said building should not be done as above, that said masters Bartolomeus or Antonius shall not have said salary of said three florins per month during said time.

---

[3] The architect Antonio da San Gallo the Elder was then working with Baccio d'Agnolo on the Florentine cathedral, and he was his senior by nine years.

INDEX

Abelard, Peter, 40
Adimari family, 58
    Girolamo, 117–118
    Lodovico, 104–106
    Piero di Bernardo, 58, 117–118
Alexander VI, pope, 52
Alfonso the Wise, king of Castile and
    Léon, 37, 89–91
angels, 23, 38, 69
Anthony, saint, 49
Antoniazzo Romano, painter, 22n
Antoninus, saint, 39
Apulia, 37, 38
Aquinas, Thomas, saint, 44
archbishop of Florence, 17–18, 39, 58,
    63, 68, 70, 105–106, 110–112
Arezzo, 44n, 54, 61n
Atlas Marianus, 38n, 60
Augustine, saint, 39n, 43

Baccio d'Agnolo, architect, 64–65, 95,
    117–119
Badia Tedalda, 46
Bagno di Romagna, 61n
Baldus (Baldo degli Ubaldi), jurist, 44n
Barga, 30
Bargello. *See* Palace of the Podestà
Bartholomew of Trent, 36
Bartolommeo di Giovanni, painter, 24
Bartolus of Sassoferrato, jurist, 44n
Benivieni family, 60
    Antonio, 60
    Girolamo, 59–60, 117–118
    Michele, 60
Bernardino, saint, 39
Bertachinus (Giovanni Bertacchini),
    jurist, 44
Bibbona, 61n
Bindi, Bastiano, 47n
blasphemy, 31, 36–38, 43–50, 52, 57
Bohemia, 42n
Bologna, 29, 36, 44n, 45

Inquisition in, 36
    Podestà, 45
Bolzano, 36
bonfires of "vanities", 52
Borgia, Cesare, 53–54
Borgia, Lucrezia, 54n
Bottrigari, Jacopo, jurist, 44n
Bouthillier, Jean, jurist, 41
Brozzi, 57
Brunelleschi, Filippo, architect, 64
Buonsignori, Stefano, 65, 95
burial, 26–27, 40n, 47

Caballo, Pietro, jurist, 45n
Caesarius of Heisterbach, 40n
canon law, ecclesiastical law, 35–36,
    39–40, 43–45, 47–49, 101–102
Cantigas de Santa Maria (Alfonso the
    Wise), 37–38, 89–91
Captain, Palace of the. *See* Palace of
    the Podestà
Carnival, 52, 57
Catalonia, 38
catasti, 28n
Charles VIII, king of France, 51
Christopher, saint, 49
chronology, 14, 27
Ciompi revolt, 31, 53
Citerna, 56
civil law, Roman law, 39, 41–45, 50
Civitavecchia, 32n
Claro, Giulio, jurist, 45
Code of Justinian, 36n, 39n, 41
Comester, Peter, theologian, 44
Company of the Blacks, 18–19, 24,
    26–27, 31, 43, 50, 63, 69n,
    107–109
Company of St. Luke, 25
Company of St. Urban (San Miniato),
    19n
Company of S. Maria della Croce al
    Tempio, 19n, 107–108

Confraternity of S. Giovanni Decollato (San Miniato), 19n
Conrad IV, German king and king of Sicily and Jerusalem, 37
Corpus Christi, 38n
Cortona, 30
councils of the church
　Florence, provincial synod, 48–49
　Fourth Lateran Council, 36
　Fifth Lateran Council, 48
　Paris (1429), 47n
　Ravenna, Second Council of , 47
　Toledo, Sixteenth Council of, 39
Cronaca, architect, 56
crucifixes, 48, 50, 57
currency, 15

Dame Fortune, 36
del Badia, Iodoco, 22
del Cittadino, Francesco, 117–118
del Magno, Giovanni, 30n
del Pie, Simone di Daniello, 50
del Quadro, Piero, 47
devils, 23, 38, 40, 69
Dickens, Charles, 18n
Dolciati family, 25
　Filippo, painter, 11, 24–25, 67–68, 73–82, 115–116
　Simone di Piero di Lorenzo, 25n
Dominican order, 51–52, 56, 59
Donati, Bernardo, 117–118
Duccio di Buoninsegna, painter, 23n, 86

Eidsivathinglaw, 40n
Eight for Security. *See* Florence—courts and magistracies
Eleonora of Toledo, duchess of Florence, 47
Empoli, 30
England, 42n
ergotism, 49
Este, Alfonso I, duke of Ferrara, 54n
eyewitnesses, 42n

Fascioli, Monaldo de', 32
feast-days, 32
　Annunciation (25 March), 14
　St. John Gualbert (12 July), 56
　St. Francis (4 October), 56
　St. Mary Magdalene (22 July), 18, 32, 107, 110–114
Fermo, 44n
Ferrara, 54n
Feu, Jean (Joannes Igneus), 41
Fig Tree, tavern, 17, 22, 27, 73
Fineschi, Vincenzo, 36n
Florence—churches, monasteries
　Badia Fiorentina, 29
　Cathedral (S. Maria dei Fiori), 58, 64, 119n
　Madonna dei Ricci, 22, 24–25, 58–60, 62–71, 95–96, 98–99, 111–119
　Orsanmichele, 49
　S. Benedetto, *popolo* of, 30n
　S. Francesco al Monte alle Croci, 17, 56, 76
　S. Marco, 51, 59
　S. Maria degli Alberighi, 17, 24–25, 58–60, 62n, 63–71, 75, 94–95, 101–109,
113–114, 117–118
　S. Maria della Croce al Tempio, 26
　S. Maria Maggiore, 29
　S. Maria Novella, 28, 36
　S. Miniato, 56, 110–112
　S. Salvatore al Monte, 56
　SS. Annunziata, 60, 70–71, 100
　Temple, the, 26–27, 87, 108–109
Florence—courts, magistracies
　ambassadors, 54
　Captain of the People, 31, 33, 55
　commissioners, 54, 56
　Council of Justice, 33
　Great Council, 52–55
　Eight for Security, 17–18, 25, 27, 30–33, 35, 39n, 48, 50, 55, 63, 66, 71, 79, 101–105, 110–114
　Executor of the Ordinances of Justice, 31
　Mercanzia, 30
　Officers of the Tower, 63
　Podestà, 30–33, 55, 88, 102–103, 107, 110–112
　Ruota, 33
　Signoria, 52, 55, 64

Standard Bearer of Justice, 54
Standard Bearer of Justice for Life, 56
Ten of Liberty and Peace, 55, 56n
Florence—streets, squares, 57
    "canto de' Ricci," 24, 71, 110
    Piazza of S. Maria Novella, 36
    Piazza of the Signoria, 52, 93
    Porta San Piero, 65, 104–105
    Via dell'Alloro, 29
    Via del Corso, 66, 96
    Via de' Malcontenti, 26
    Via di Porta San Piero, 104–105
Foggia, 37
France, 41, 43n, 51, 53–54
Francesca Romana, saint, 22n
Francis, saint, 56
French disease. See syphilis
Franciscan order, 17, 52, 56, 58

Gaddi, Taddeo, painter, 62
Gaeta, 49
gambling, 17, 31, 35–39, 45, 49, 52, 57
Germany, German, 37
Giacomini, Antonio, 56
Giambiglioni, Angelo, jurist, 44n
Giovanni da Milano, painter, 62
Giovanni di Simone, smith, 66–67
Giuliani, Bernardo di messer Lelio,
    108–109
Giuseppe (as baptismal name), 26
God's cuckold, 26
Good Thief, the, 23
grandi, 52–55
Gregory the Great, saint and pope, 44
Gualbert, John, saint, 56
Guibert of Nogent, 40
Guicciardini, Francesco, 42n, 53n
Gumppenberg, Wilhelm, 60

hat of infamy (mitra infamiae), 48
Heloise, 40
homosexuality, 52, 57
house-scorning, 43

iconoclasm, 12
Imola, 44n
incest, 37

intent, criminal, 39–42

James, saint, 40
Jesus Christ, 21, 23, 46–48, 57
Jews, 31, 49
Joan of Arc, 42n
Joseph, saint, 26
Julian, sixth-century jurist, 44
Juno, goddess, 71n
Justinian, emperor, 39n, 44

La Verna, 56
Lady Luck, 36
laesa maiestas, 43
laesa religio, 43
Landi, Giovanni di Piero, 20, 104, 115,
    117–118
Landucci, Luca, 20–22, 25, 27, 31, 49,
    63, 65, 110
Lapini, Agostino, 21
Last Judgment, 23
laymen, 36, 62
lay piety, 60–62
Lent, 52, 57
Leviticus, 44
lex Cornelia, 41
Limoges, 58n
Lippi, Filippino, painter, 23n, 85
Livy (Titus Livius), 71n
lynching, 17, 49

Machiavelli, Niccolò, 52n, 55n, 71n
Madonna de' Ricci
    fresco and tabernacle, 17–18, 22,
        24–25, 43, 58–71, 75, 97–99,
        101–114
    oratory. See Florence—churches and
        monasteries
    opera of, 20, 24, 58–60, 63–71, 104,
        115–119
madonnieri, 25
magnate families, 28, 55
Mantua, 49
Mappa della Catena, 26n, 87
marrano, 49
Martin of Tours, saint, 40
Martino of Brozzi, 57

Mary, saint (also "the Virgin"), 35–38, 43, 47–50, 58, 61–62, 69–71
  images of, 36–38, 48–50, 61–62, 69–71
  Mariology, 58
  See also Madonna de' Ricci
Mary Magdalene, saint. *See* feast-days
Medici family, 51–52, 59
  Cosimo I, duke of Florence and grand duke of Tuscany, 47
  Ferdinand II, grand duke of Tuscany, 60
  Francesco, grand duke of Tuscany, 65n
  Lorenzo the Magnificent, 51–52, 60
  Lucrezia. *See* Salviati Medici
  Piero di Lorenzo, 51
Mini, Giovan Battista de', 67, 68n
Modigliana, 45
Montepulciano, 30, 61n

Naldini family, 28
  Francesco di Domenico, 28n
Naples, 61n
Niccolò di Baldo, 68–69
nobles, noblemen, 28, 48, 73

observantism, observancy, 51, 56, 58, 110–112
Old Testament, 43, 45
opera. *See* Madonna de' Ricci
Onophrius, saint, 49
oratory. *See* Madonna de' Ricci
Origen, 40, 43n
Original Sin, the, 23
Orvieto, 32
ottimati, 52, 54. *See also grandi*

Pagni, Lorenzo, 45n
Palace of the Podestà (also Palace of the Captain, Bargello), 17–18, 21n, 26, 32, 81, 84, 102–105, 107, 110–112
Palace of the Signoria, 64
Pandolfini, Bartolomeo, 59, 117–118
Pazzi, Geri di Poldo, 68n
Penitential of Vigila of Avila, 39–40
Peter, saint, 23, 85
Peter of Belleperche, jurist, 41
Phillip IV, king of France, 41
Pietà, painted by Dolciati, 24, 115–116

Pietrasanta, 47n
Pisa, 37, 46, 49, 53
Pistoia, 50, 55, 61n, 71n
pitture infamanti, 21, 84
popolo, popolare, 28n, 52–55
Portugal, 38n
poverty, poor relief, 42n, 46n, 48
Prato, 28, 30, 61n
Prophets, painted by Dolciati, 24, 115–116
Protestant Reformation, 12
Prussia, 42n
Pugliese, Francesco di Filippo del, 59, 117–118

Ricci family, 59
  Giorgio di Piero, 117–118
  Rosso de', 24, 62
  Uguccio de', 117–118
Richa, Giuseppe, 20, 68
Rinaldeschi family, 28–30
  Alessandra (mother of Antonio), 29, 30n
  Angela (stepmother of A.), 29, 30n
  Antonia (grandmother of A.), 30
  Antonia (half-sister of A.), 30n
  Antonio di Giovanni, 17–18, 20, 23, 25–31, 101–114
  Antonio (c. 1400), 28–29
  Bartholomeo di Giovanni di Bindo, 29n
  Bartolommea (stepmother of A.), 29, 30n
  Biagio di Giovanni di Biagio, 29n
  Giovanni (c. 1400), 29
  Giovanni di Antonio (father of A.), 26, 29, 30n
  Giovanni di Arrigaccio, 28n
  Lucrezia (half-sister of A.), 29n
  Rinaldo di Dego, 28n
Roger, twelfth-century jurist, 44
Roman law. *See* civil law
Rome, 22n, 52, 57
Rustici codex, 62n, 94

sacrilege, 38, 43–50
Saint Anthony's fire, 49
saints, 23, 46–47
Salviati, Jacopo, 60
Salviati Medici, Lucrezia, 60, 112

San Miniato codex, 19, 27, 69
Sangallo, Antonio da, architect, 65, 117–119
Savelli, Marco Antonio, jurist, 45
Savonarola, Girolamo, 32, 35, 42, 49, 51–53, 55–60, 70, 92–93
Scala, Antonio di Bartolomeo, 54n
scapegoat, 31
Scolopi Fathers, 60
Segaloni, Francesco, 20n
Segaloni, Matteo, architect, 20, 21n, 113–114
Servite order, 52, 60n
Soderini family, 53–54
Giovanvittorio, 53, 54n
Paolantonio, 53, 54n
Piero, 53–54, 56, 64
Tommaso, 54n
sodomy. *See* homosexuality
Spain, 38n, 39–40

Strozzi, Carlo, 21, 111–112
suicide, 17, 35, 39–42
syphilis, 20, 31, 113–114

Tartagni, Alessandro, jurist, 44n, 45
treason, 43
Trent, 36
Tor de' Specchi, 22n
torture, 42n, 52
Toschi, Domenico, jurist, 44–45

Uccello, Paolo, painter, 22n

Valdichiana, 54
Venice, 46n
vicar of the archbishop, 18, 58, 63, 68, 104–106

wax offerings, 63, 70, 110–112
Winchester, 49

Publications of the
Centre for Reformation and Renaissance Studies

ISBN information is for paperback edition unless otherwise specified

Barnabe Riche Society Publications

Lodge, Thomas. *A Margarite of America*. Ed. by Henry Janzen and intro. by Don Beecher (2005), pp. 205. ISBN 0-7727-2027-4

Essays and Studies

Sins of the Flesh: Responding to Sexual Disease in Early Modern Europe. Ed. Kevin Siena (2005), pp. 296. ISBN 0-7727-2029-0

Zirpolo, Lilian. *Ave Papa, Ave Papabile: The Sacchetti Family, Their Art Patronage, and Political Aspirations*. (2005), pp. 252. ISBN 0-7727-2028-2

Fantasies of Troy: Classical Tales and the Social Imaginary in Medieval and Early Modern Europe. Ed. by Alan Shepard and Stephen D. Powell (2004), pp. 306. ISBN 0-7727-2025-8

Shell Games: Studies in Scams, Frauds, and Deceits (1300-1650) Ed. by Mark Crane, Richard Raiswell and Margaret Reeves (2004), pp.334. ISBN 0-7727-2023-1

A Renaissance of Conflicts: Visions and Revisions of Law and Society in Italy and Spain. Ed. by John Marino and Thomas Kuehn (2004), pp. 456. ISBN 0-7727-2022-3

The Renaissance in the Nineteenth Century / Le XIXe siècle renaissant. Ed. by Yannick Portebois and Nicolas Terpstra (2003), pp. 302. ISBN 0-7727-2019-3

The Premodern Teenager: Youth in Society 1150-1650. Ed. by Konrad Eisenbichler (2002), pp. 349. ISBN 0-7727-2018-5

Occasional Publications

Estes, James M. *The First Forty Years: A Brief History of the Centre for Reformation and Renaissance Studies*. (2004), pp. 106. ISBN 0-7727-2026-6

Annotated Catalogue of Editions of Erasmus at the Centre for Reformation and Renaissance Studies, Toronto. Comp. by Jacqueline Glomski and Erika Rummel (1994), pp. 153. ISBN 0-9697512-1-4

Register of Sermons Preached at St. Paul's Cross (1534-1642). Comp. by Millar MacLure and revised by Peter Pauls and Jackson Campbell Boswell (1989), pp. 152. ISBN 0-919473-48-2

Language and Literature. Early Printed Books at the CRRS. Comp. by Willian R. Bowen and Konrad Eisenbichler (1986), pp. 112. ISBN 0-7727-2009-6

Published Books (1499-1700) on Science, Medicine and Natural History at the CRRS Comp. by William R. Bowen and Konrad Eisenbichler (1986), pp. 37. ISBN 0-7727-2005-3

Bibles, Theological Treatises and Other Religious Literature, 1492-1700, at the CRRS. Comp. by Konrad Eisenbichler, Gay MacDonald and Robert Sweetman (1981), pp. 94. ISBN 0-7727-2002-9

Humanist Editions of Statutes and Histories at the CRRS. Comp. by Konrad Eisenbichler, Gay MacDonald and C. Turner (1980), pp. 63. ISBN 0-7727-2001-0

Humanist Editions of the Classics at the CRRS. Comp. N.L. Anderson, Kenneth R. Bartlett, Konrad Eisenbichler, and Janis Svilpis (1979), pp. 71. ISBN 0-7727-2000-2

Renaissance and Reformation Texts in Translation

Du Bellay, Ronsard, Sébillet. *Poetry and Language in 16ᵗʰ-Century France.* Trans. and intro. by Laura Willett (2004), pp.116. ISBN 0-7727-2021-5

Girolamo Savonarola. *A Guide to Righteous Living and Other Works.* Trans. and intro. by Konrad Eisenbichler (2003), pp. 243. ISBN 0-7727-2020-7

Godly Magistrates and Church Order: Johannes Brenz and the Establishment of the Lutheran Territorial Church in Germany, 1524-1559. Trans. and ed. by James M. Estes (2001), pp. 219. ISBN 0-7727-2017-7

Giovanni Della Casa. *Galateo: A Renaissance Treatise on Manners.* Trans. by Konrad Eisenbichler and Kenneth R. Bartlett. 3ʳᵈ ed. (2001), pp. 98. ISBN 0-9697512-2-2

Romeo and Juliet Before Shakespeare: Four Stories of Star-Crossed Love. Trans. by Nicole Prunster (2000), pp. 127. ISBN 0-7727-2015-0

Jean Bodin. *On the Demon-Mania of Witches.* Abridged, trans. and ed. Randy A. Scott and Jonathan L. Pearl (1995), pp. 219. ISBN 0-9697512-5-7

Whether Secular Government Has the Right to Wield the Sword in Matters of Faith: A Controversy in Nürnberg in 1530. Trans. and ed. by James M. Estes (1994), pp. 118. ISBN 0-9697512-4-9

Lorenzo Valla. *'The Profession of the Religious' and Selections from 'The Falsely-Believed and Forged Donation of Constantine'.* Trans. and ed. Olga Z. Pugliese. 2ⁿᵈ ed. (1994), pp. 114. ISBN 0-9697512-3-0

A. Karlstadt, H. Emser, J. Eck. *A Reformation Debate: Karlstadt, Emser and Eck on Sacred Images.* Trans. and ed. Brian Mangrum and Giuseppe Scavizzi. 2ⁿᵈ edition (1991), pp. 112. ISBN 0-9697512-7-3

Nicholas of Cusa. *The Layman on Wisdom and the Mind.* Trans. Mark L. Feuhrer (1989), pp. 112. ISBN 0-919473-56-3

Bernardino Ochino. *Seven Dialogues.* Trans. and ed. Rita Belladonna (1988), pp. 96. ISBN 0-919473-63-6

Tudor and Stuart Texts

The Queen's Majesty's Passage and Related Documents. Ed. and intro by Germaine Warkentin. (2004), pp. 158. ISBN 0-7727-2024-X

Early Stuart Pastoral: 'The Shepherd's Pipe' by William Browne and others, and *'The Shepherd's Hunting' by George Wither.* Ed. and intro by James Doelman (1999), pp. 196. ISBN 0-9697512-9-X

The Trial of Nicholas Throckmorton. Ed. and intro by Annabel Patterson (1998), pp. 108. ISBN 0-9697512-8-1

James I. *The True Law of Free Monarchies* and *Basilikon Doron.* Ed. and intro by Daniel Fischlin and Mark Fortier (1996), pp. 181. ISBN 0-9697512-6-5

To order books, and for additional information, contact:
CRRS Publications, Victoria University
71 Queen's Park, Toronto ON, M5S 1K7, CANADA
tel: (416) 585-4465 / fax: (416) 585-4430
e-mail: crrs.publications@utoronto.ca / web: <www.crrs.ca>

MEMBRE DU GROUPE SCABRINI

Québec, Canada
2005